I0876624

The 7 Habits of Financially Healthy Women

Books by Crystal Paine
from Bethany House Publishers

Love-Centered Parenting

The Time-Saving Mom

The 7 Habits of Financially Healthy Women

The 7 Habits of Financially Healthy Women

HOW TO STOP STRESSING,
BEGIN WHERE YOU ARE,
AND BUILD THE FUTURE YOU WANT

CRYSTAL PAINE

BETHANYHOUSE
a division of Baker Publishing Group
Minneapolis, Minnesota

Published by Bethany House Publishers
Minneapolis, Minnesota
BethanyHouse.com

Bethany House Publishers is a division of
Baker Publishing Group, Grand Rapids, Michigan

Printed in the United States of America

Library of Congress Cataloging-in-Publication Data
Names: Paine, Crystal author
Title: The 7 habits of financially healthy women : how to stop stressing, begin where you are, and build the future you want / Crystal Paine.
Other titles: Seven habits of financially healthy women
Description: Minneapolis, Minnesota : Bethany House, a division of Baker Publishing Group, [2026] | Includes bibliographical references.
Identifiers: LCCN 2026014745 | ISBN 9780764237263 paperback | ISBN 9781493455423 ebook
Subjects: LCSH: Women—Finance, Personal | Finance, Personal
Classification: LCC HG179 .P176 2026
LC record available at https://lccn.loc.gov/2026014745

Scripture quotations are from the King James Version of the Bible.

Cover design by Alecia Sharp

Baker Publishing Group publications use paper produced from sustainable forestry practices and postconsumer waste whenever possible.

26 27 28 29 30 31 32 7 6 5 4 3 2 1

Contents

Introduction 7

Why This Works 13
The Compound Effect of Small Choices

Habit #1 Start with What You Have 31
Do What You Can, with What You Have, Where You Are

Habit #2 Decide Your Financial Priorities 55
Name Your Why and Set Your Compass

Habit #3 Predetermine Your Spending 77
Set Up a Money Plan (aka Budget) in Under an Hour

Habit #4 Use Cash for Everything 111
Spend Only the Money You Already Have

Habit #5 Create Irresistible Accountability 131
Identify Your Style and Tailor a Plan That Works for You

Habit #6 Stop Paying Full Price 153
Shift from Passive Spender to Strategic Steward

Habit #7 Consult Your Ninety-Year-Old Self 191
Build Your Legacy on Change, Humility, and Hope

Notes 203

Introduction

My heart was pounding. My chest felt tight. My skin felt clammy.

I had been going over the numbers in my head repeatedly and I was starting to feel panicked.

We had been married for almost five years. We had a toddler and a newborn. I had just walked through some scary health issues (more on that in the next chapter). Our bank account was quickly dwindling. And there wasn't enough money coming in to cover our monthly expenses.

My husband, Jesse, had graduated from law school and then, due to things outside our control, our neat little plan for the next five years of our lives had gone up in smoke.

The good job he was supposed to have for a few years after law school didn't pan out. So we scrambled to find an alternative and ended up moving suddenly when another job opened up in a city an hour away.

But then that job turned out to not be at all what we'd hoped, and it lasted only a short while.

So there we were with two little kids, a dangerously low bank balance, no job, and a lot of bills.

It was scary. Honestly, many days it felt more than scary; I think *terrifying* is a more appropriate word.

Maybe you've felt that same breathless fear when it comes to your finances—the one that tightens your chest and makes everything blur around you.

Maybe that's exactly why you picked up this book. Because the financial pressure feels heavy right now, and you're not just scared about your future: There are many moments when you feel downright terrified.

Perhaps you've found yourself lying awake at night, running the numbers in your head, feeling overwhelmed by and anxious about all the what-ifs and unknowns, wondering how in the world you're going to make ends meet and worried what tomorrow and the next few months might hold. You may have even thought, *Am I going to make it?*

You Are Not Alone in Your Money Worries

As I was writing this book, I surveyed nearly four thousand women and asked them to anonymously share their greatest fears around money. You know what surprised me most about the results of the survey?

Almost every woman—whether she was barely scraping by or was doing well financially—admitted that she was carrying some level of fear when it came to money or that she felt some uncertainty about her financial future.

Whether you are feeling paralyzed by panic over the unknowns of the future or maybe just mildly worried over where you are financially, I want you to know you are not alone!

Let me share just a few of the most common fears women said they wrestle with. As you read, put a checkmark next to the ones that sound familiar to you:

"There are too many bills and not enough income."

"I feel stretched thin. There's never enough time, never enough money."

"I feel this heavy weight that I won't be able to give my kids the life I want for them."

"What if something terrible happens and wipes out our savings?

"I make decent money, so why doesn't it feel like enough?"

"I wish I felt more confident about my financial future."

If you saw yourself in any of those statements, I want you to know two things:

1. **You are not alone.** (Yes, that bears repeating.)
2. **You are in the right place.**

I hope this list helps you feel *seen* and encouraged. Because the truth is, while most women carry some kind of financial fear, far too few of us talk about it.

And that's exactly why I wrote this book.

I want to walk alongside you like a friend with a flashlight, helping you shine a light on your finances—without judgment, without shame, and with lots of grace. Think of me as your cheerleader and guide, here to give you practical steps, simple encouragement, and just enough of a loving nudge to help you move forward.

Why Trust Me?

I've been blogging about saving money for over twenty years (come hang out with us at MoneySavingMom.com for daily deals and encouragement!), but in this book, I want to take you back before all that. Before the website. Before the books. Before the podcast. Before Instagram.

Back to the little girl watching her parents work hard, save diligently, pay off their house, and build a debt-free life—one decision at a time.

You'll hear stories from those years—about living in an old construction trailer with no oven or air conditioning, battling mice infestations, and having windows that leaked like faucets when it rained. You'll also see how my parents' quiet commitment to living below their means planted seeds in my heart that would later grow into one of the boldest decisions my husband and I ever made: to live debt-free from day one of our marriage.

I'll share how we stretched our dollars when money was so tight in our early years of being married. And by tight, I really mean that. We sometimes had only seventeen to twenty dollars to buy all of our groceries for all the meals for the week for the two of us.

You'll see how those tiny choices turned into big changes over time. I won't sugarcoat the truth: It required a lot of sacrifices, and there were many hard seasons (like the one I shared at the beginning of this introduction).

But I am here—years later—to tell you that the little habits we established early in our marriage have yielded a harvest of financial fruit. And I believe the same can prove true for you!

In the pages ahead, I'll equip you with the tools and strategies that helped us shift from barely scraping by to thriving. I want you, too, to feel confident, purposeful, and excited about your financial future.

Whether you're hoping for just a few good money-saving ideas or you are looking for a complete financial overhaul, I wrote this for you. It's not just a collection of stories or tips. It's a blueprint for building a legacy—one small, faithful step at a time.

Here's How We'll Do It

I truly believe with all my heart that you, yes you, can achieve financial health. Even if you feel like you've failed in the past and you don't have good money skills or financial discipline, that does not change my belief. Because here's the truth: **Today is a new day.**

In the chapters that follow, I will help you:

- **Conquer the fear and limiting beliefs** that whisper you "just aren't good with money," "aren't disciplined enough," or "never follow through."
- **Craft a personalized road map** for long-term financial health—one that fits your unique personality, priorities, and purpose.
- **Create a flexible daily and weekly plan** that gives you space to meet your financial goals *and still* enjoy your life, save for the future, and invest in the causes you care about.
- **Cultivate irresistible accountability** that keeps you consistent and committed, even on the hard days—because lasting change thrives in community.

So take a deep breath, friend. You've already taken the first brave step by opening this book.

My greatest desire is that these pages will spark fresh life and renewed excitement in your financial journey. That you'll find practical tools, new inspiration, and most of all, **hope.**

No matter your current situation . . .

No matter your income or job . . .

No matter your background, education, or where you live . . .

You *can* live a financially healthy life.

Why This Works

The Compound Effect of Small Choices

I walked into the bathroom expecting to take a routine test. I had no idea it was about to turn my world upside down for the next few weeks.

It was 2007. I was 34 weeks pregnant with our second child.

My midwife had come to our house for what I thought was just another standard prenatal checkup, nothing out of the ordinary. But that seemingly simple appointment would be the beginning of a whirlwind of unexpected events.

Just like I had done during every other visit, I headed to the bathroom to pee in the little cup so my midwife could run the routine pregnancy screenings she did at every visit.

But this time, something wasn't right.

She looked at the results—and immediately picked up the phone. Within minutes, we were on our way to the hospital. I was admitted on the spot.

Things moved so quickly that my brain could barely keep up. Words like *leukemia* were suddenly being whispered. My hospital room became a revolving door of doctors and nurses asking urgent questions and drawing vial after vial of blood.

That first night, I lay in the hospital bed alone—my husband home with our toddler—and I couldn't sleep. I tossed and turned, mind racing, heart pounding.

I felt so scared—not just for the baby growing inside me, but for what this might mean for all of us.

What if I had a life-threatening illness?

What if I had only months left to live?

How would my husband manage with two little ones without me?

What kind of trauma would this bring to our family?

I was so young. My husband needed me. My babies needed me. My mind was spiraling.

After days in the hospital undergoing tests and being seen by dozens of medical professionals—with a whole lot of frightening words being tossed around—the results finally came in. And what did the doctors find?

No life-threatening illness. No cancer. No mystery condition. Just a very severe case of pregnancy-induced anemia.

My platelet count and hemoglobin were dangerously low, and my body had gone into crisis mode. The cause? Not some fluke or a freak condition. It was a slow deterioration, the result of my not taking care of myself for months.

Yes, being pregnant contributed to it. And yes, that season of life was full of challenges. But the truth was undeniable: I had been neglecting my health.

Skipping meals. Skimping on sleep. Living in a constant state of exhaustion. Ignoring the signs my body was giving me to slow down and rest.

It wasn't one big decision; it was dozens of little ones, day after day, that added up to my body finally crying, "Enough!"

Ultimately, my labor was induced early, and I gave birth to a strong, healthy baby girl—our second daughter. With rest and attention, my body healed. My blood work returned to more normal ranges. And I was pronounced back to full health.

That was nearly two decades ago, but I've never forgotten the lessons I learned lying in that hospital bed. Once I was well again, I made a decision: I was going to start paying attention.

Not only to my physical health, but to the small, seemingly insignificant choices that add up to big results over time.

I started on a journey to better health. I began to eat more iron-rich foods, tried not to skip meals (especially breakfast), prioritized sleep more, increased my exercise, made time for rest and relaxation, cut back some on my workload . . . and I began paying more attention to the little indications my body would give me that things were not okay or were starting to get out of whack.

Because little choices matter. And the same is true when it comes to your finances.

In the moment, it might feel like our daily choices aren't making much of a difference.

But over time? They matter more than we realize.

When small actions are repeated consistently, they compound into something powerful—whether in our health, our relationships, or our finances.

Sure, there are always factors in life that are outside our control. Genetics, age, the economy, the job market, the cost of living—they all play a part. But even with those realities, there's still *so much* we can take ownership of.

This is just as true with our financial health as it is with our physical health.

The choices we make with money on a daily basis don't just impact the here and now. They shape our future.

As I recounted in the introduction, we've had our fair share of difficult financial seasons. We've lived on very little. We've had months when there was almost nothing in the bank account, and our meager income was not enough to cover anything but the most basic of basics.

It was during those times that our commitment to healthy financial habits mattered most. In fact, I look back years later and realize that those months and years when money was so tight and we chose to make a lot of sacrifices and forgo so many purchases and make do with what we had . . . those little daily choices laid the foundation for where we are today.

Note: I know that not all choices are made on a level playing field. Sometimes, what looks like a poor decision from the outside really was the best option available in the moment. If you can relate to this, know that I'm over here cheering for you as you take one small baby step at a time in building your financial health!

So What Is Financial Health?

The fact that you're reading this book tells me that you're being intentional about building a future that's financially healthy. (I'm so proud of you!) But the truth is that a lot of us didn't have the opportunity to see what financial health looked like when we were growing up.

Maybe you were raised by a single parent who had limited job opportunities but worked hard to make ends meet.

Or maybe you were raised by parents who *made enough*, but spent their money recklessly as soon as it came in.

Or perhaps you grew up financially comfortable and had caregivers who were largely responsible with their money, but you never saw them being thoughtful in their spending; maybe they were very stingy when it came to spending money on others and didn't practice generosity.

A lot of us haven't had the opportunity to see what financial health and responsibility looks like.

So before we get any further in the book, let's define what financial health is. Because if I'm going to teach you habits that add up to financial health, I think you probably first want to know what financial health *is*!

Here's my definition: Financial health is the quiet confidence and calm that comes from managing your money with intention. It is seeing money as a tool to bring freedom instead of fear. It is being in a position where money serves your life instead of running your life.

Financial health does not mean you've achieved a certain standard of living or have a predetermined amount of money in your bank account. Rather, it's your mindset around money. It's viewing your finances with clarity and purpose and having a plan for your financial future that gives you calm instead of chaos.

Financially healthy women intentionally build and maintain habits that help them live within their means, prepare for the future, and give generously—starting right where they are, with what they have.

What Financial Health Isn't

Being financially healthy does not mean you have to

have a high income. You can have a strong income and still live paycheck to paycheck. Conversely, you can have a modest income and thrive financially.

be completely debt-free. Many people are financially healthy while still paying off a mortgage, student loans, or other debt.

be an expert at financial lingo. You don't need to be a finance whiz to make wise, healthy money choices.

- **never spend money on fun or frivolous things.** Being financially healthy means making space for joy without guilt.
- **stick to a budget meticulously and rigidly every month.** A healthy financial life allows for flexibility, life changes, and grace when plans shift.
- **own a home.** Contrary to what many will tell you, I believe it can sometimes be a smart financial decision to rent a home instead of buy one.
- **have a big savings account balance right now.** Financial health starts with intentional small steps. It's not dependent upon having a hefty chunk of money in the bank.
- **be ridiculously frugal or restrictive.** Financially healthy people spend on what matters to them and cut back on what doesn't.
- **have a stable income.** Many people with variable or freelance income still manage money in healthy, confident ways. (By the way, my husband and I never had set income. Due to owning our own businesses and having jobs with varying hours, our income has always fluctuated from month to month.)
- **never make mistakes.** Everyone makes money mistakes—financial health means learning from them, not living in shame over them.

The Road to Financial Health

The road to financial health begins with setting attainable goals and creating a simple, sustainable game plan to reach them. Goals are what guide you as you begin to take small, purposeful steps forward.

Maybe your goal is to save to pay cash for a new car in two years.

Maybe your goal is to save up for your child to attend a state university a decade from now.

Or maybe your goal is to retire by sixty so you can spend more time volunteering with a nonprofit doing incredible work in the world.

Whatever it is, don't underestimate the power of a clear financial goal. Why? Because setting goals gives your financial habits purpose, direction, and staying power.

Without a goal, it's easy to lose motivation. But when you know *why* you're saying no to impulse purchases or yes to packing lunches instead of eating out, the sacrifice feels meaningful. It gives you perspective that makes it easier to stay consistent, even when progress feels slow.

Goals also create accountability. Writing them down and reviewing them regularly keeps you focused and honest. It's a lot harder to splurge on something unnecessary when you've got a list of meaningful priorities hanging on your fridge or tucked into your journal.

And perhaps most importantly, goals build momentum. When you track your progress—especially in small monthly steps—you start to see growth. Even if you hit a setback or unexpected expense, those written goals remind you that you *are* making progress, even if it's slower than you'd hoped. That is often the nudge you need to keep going.

So I encourage you to set your sights on a goal that truly matters to you and then use the *Seven Habits of Financially Healthy Women* to build your path toward it. These habits will help you stay intentional, motivated, and equipped for the journey ahead.

Your Daily Choices Matter More Than You Think

So often, we make little choices without much thought of the long-term impact. We're going to be talking a lot in the pages that follow about how our simple habits and decisions add up over time—in either a positive way or a negative one.

I want to illustrate this with a simple example as we begin this journey together, one involving something all of us likely consume every day: water.

I'm a firm believer that staying hydrated is one of the easiest ways to care for your health, so I try to drink plenty of water every day. There are multiple options for obtaining water, and it might not seem like it matters much. But let's run the numbers.

- **Filling up a water bottle at home:**
  Approximately $0.03 per day × 365 days = **$10.95** per year
- **Grabbing a plastic bottle from a store-bought 24-pack:**
  Approximately $0.16 per day × 365 days = **$58.40** per year
- **Buying a single bottle from a vending machine or gas station:**
  Approximately $1.79 per day × 365 days = **$653.35** per year

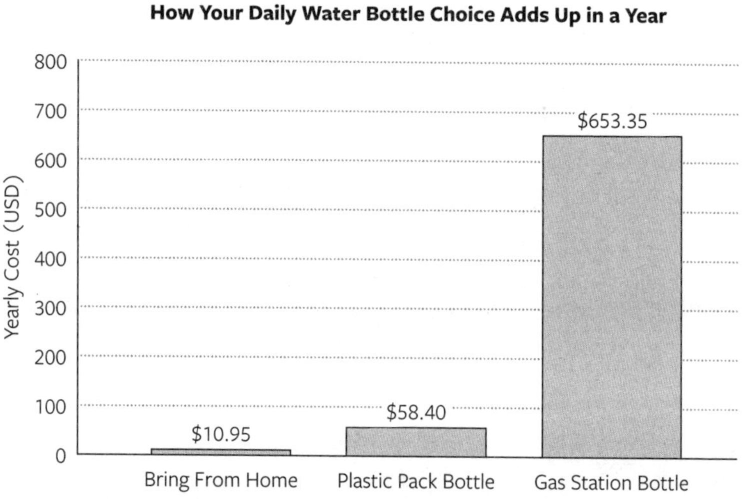

Yes, you read that right. The difference between grabbing a water bottle at a gas station every day when you are out and about or filling up a water bottle at home adds up to **over $650 per year.**

And over forty years? That simple habit could save you **more than $26,000!!!**

All from filling up a reusable water bottle each morning.

Now, I'm not telling you this to guilt you if you've ever bought a $1.79 water bottle. (I've done it too!) I'm sharing it to open your eyes to something empowering:

Your little choices aren't so little after all.

Small Purchases That Can Add Up Over Time

Buying a bottle of water can feel like such a small purchase—and it is! But over time, purchasing a water bottle again and again can add up to a lot of money spent. Maybe you don't buy bottled water, but perhaps there are other small purchases you often make that could add up in the same way:

- Daily coffee shop drinks
- Drive-thru or takeout meals
- App store purchases (games, upgrades, subscriptions)
- Streaming service subscriptions you rarely use
- Snacks or gum at checkout lines
- Impulse buys from online sales or social media ads
- Monthly subscription boxes
- ATM fees or banking fees
- Late fees or small interest charges
- Delivery fees and tips for frequent orders
- Gas station add-ons (drinks, snacks, lottery tickets)
- Cheap clothing or accessories "just because"
- In-app purchases for entertainment or kids
- Unused memberships (gyms, apps, subscriptions)
- "Bargain" finds that weren't planned and aren't needed

When you start thinking in these terms, you realize just how much power you hold in your daily habits. One small shift can lead to significant long-term results.

That's the kind of mindset we're going to build together in this book—creating sustainable, healthy habits around your finances that may not feel huge in the moment but will add up to something *life-changing* over time.

Simple, Proven Strategies Followed Consistently = Long-Term Success

My heart is to walk alongside you and hand you a clear, doable road map—full of simple, proven strategies that may seem small at first glance but, when done consistently, can radically transform your financial future.

These strategies aren't complicated. They're not going to promise overnight riches or a one-size-fits-all system. But they *will* help you build a strong financial foundation, brick by brick, habit by habit.

In the pages ahead, we'll unpack seven key habits I believe are essential for any woman who wants to experience lasting financial health and freedom.

The Seven Habits of Financially Healthy Women

Habit #1: Start with What You Have

It's easy to believe financial peace starts with more—more income, more knowledge, more opportunity. But the best place to begin? Right where you are. In this chapter, I'll help you identify what you already have, show you how to make the most of it, and empower you to stop feeling stuck and start moving forward right away.

Habit #2: Decide Your Financial Priorities

Before you can move forward with confidence, you need to know what you're moving toward. What does financial health actually look like for you? In this chapter, we'll take a close look at the patterns, habits, and mindsets that may be holding you back. Then, I'll guide you in mapping out a new, purposeful path forward. With that fresh clarity, you'll define your personal financial priorities and lay a strong foundation for the habits to come.

Habit #3: Predetermine Your Spending

Living with financial intention means telling your money where to go instead of wondering where it went. If the idea of budgeting makes you feel a sense of dread or panic, don't worry—you're not alone. Now that you've determined your financial priorities, I'll walk you through how to create a plan for your money that feels empowering (not restrictive!) and actually gets you excited about where your dollars are going.

Habit #4: Use Cash for Everything

This one can feel a little polarizing! Rest assured, I'm not going to insist you shred your credit cards or walk around with bulging envelopes of cash for every purchase. Here's what I *am* going to challenge you to do: Focus on spending only the money you actually have (in the bank or in cash), instead of buying things with money you *hope* will come in later. This chapter is all about hitting the reset button on your spending habits. You might be surprised at how quickly your mindset shifts and how much freedom you find in building healthier patterns with your money.

Habit #5: Create Irresistible Accountability

Let's be honest: It's easy to set goals. It's much harder to follow through. That's where accountability comes in—not the guilt-trip kind, but the kind that motivates you and energizes you to keep showing up. I'll help you build support systems and rhythms that make it much easier to stick with your financial intentions, especially on the hard days.

Habit #6: Stop Paying Full Price

Now we're getting to the fun stuff! I'll share some of my very favorite strategies for saving thousands of dollars a year. From creative hacks to mindset shifts, this is where you'll learn how to train yourself to *almost never* pay full price again and actually enjoy the process.

Habit #7: Consult Your Ninety-Year-Old Self

We'll end the book with a powerful habit: living today with your future in mind. What will matter most when you're ninety? What will you wish you had spent your time, energy, and money on? We'll talk about how to align your financial decisions with what truly matters. I promise, it won't be morbid; it will be life-giving.

How's Your Financial Health? A Fun and Real-Life Money Quiz for Women

Before we dive in, let me ask you something.

Have you ever gone to a new doctor and been handed a mountain of paperwork to fill out before your appointment? Yep, me too! And I'll admit, it's not my favorite part. (Why does every form feel like an exam on my entire family's medical history? Honestly, I can barely remember my own zip code, let alone whether my great-grandma had lymphangioleiomyomatosis!)

Instead of paperwork, we're going to do something a little more fun and a whole lot more insightful.

Let's kick things off with a quick quiz to help you assess your current financial health. The goal of this quiz is to bring awareness, not shame. The first step to making changes in our lives is to realize where we are. So just answer honestly and see if there's anything you learn in the process.

How's Your Financial Health?

A Real-Life Money Quiz for Women

Don't overthink it! Go with your first instinct.

1. **When payday rolls around, what's your first move?**
   A) I have a plan for my money. My budget tells every dollar where to go.
   B) I pay my bills, buy a few things I've been eyeing, and hope there's something left.
   C) My paycheck is basically gone before I know it. How does money disappear so fast?!

2. **How do you feel when you check your bank account?**
   A) Confident and in control. I know exactly how much is in there.
   B) A little anxious, but I usually have a pretty good idea of how much I'm spending and saving.
   C) I avoid checking my bank account. I'd rather not look, as it stresses me out to know.

3. **Your best friend invites you on a weekend girls' trip, but it's not in the budget. What do you do?**
   A) Check my savings account and see if I can swing it without derailing my goals.

B) Put it on my credit card and figure it out later.

C) Say yes right away—you only live once!

4. How often do you use a budget or spending plan?

A) Every month. And I pretty much always stick to it.

B) I create one sometimes, but don't usually follow through.

C) Budget? Nope! I'm out!

5. What's your current savings situation?

A) I have an emergency fund and a detailed list of savings goals I'm working toward.

B) I try to save when I can, but unexpected expenses often throw me off.

C) The thought of setting aside money for savings sounds impossible and restrictive.

6. When it comes to debt, which best describes you?

A) I'm debt-free or have a concrete plan I'm working on to pay it off as quickly as possible.

B) I usually make minimum payments every month and call it good.

C) I don't know how much I owe. Thinking about it gives me anxiety.

7. How do you handle impulse purchases?

A) I rarely make impulse purchases. I plan ahead when I want something.

B) Sometimes I splurge, but I try to keep it reasonable, nothing over-the-top.

C) If I see it and want it, I buy it. I'll deal with figuring out how to pay for it later.

8. What's your approach to giving?

A) Generosity is a high priority in my budget and something I plan for every month.

B) I give when I can, but many months I don't have extra to make it happen.

C) I want to give, but I'm trying so hard to just make ends meet.

9. How prepared are you for a financial emergency?

A) I have three to six months of expenses set aside for emergencies.

B) I could handle a small emergency, but a big one would be tough.

C) I'd have to rely on credit or family for help if I had a financial emergency.

10. When you think about your financial future, how do you feel?

A) Hopeful and excited! I am looking forward to continuing to work toward my financial goals.

B) A little overwhelmed, but I'm trying to be more careful with my finances.

C) Stressed and unsure how I'll ever get to a place where I'm not feeling financially behind.

Your Financial Health Score

Mostly *A's*:

You are *intentional*, *goal-driven*, and *proactive*. You're making smart money moves and building a strong foundation for the future! In this book, you'll love the parts where we dive deeper into how your strong start can become a launching pad to greater impact, more freedom, and bold generosity. I can't wait to see what's next for you!

Mostly *B's*:
You've got a good start but there's room to grow. And you're right where you need to be! This book will help you fill in the gaps, tweak your habits, and finally feel confident and in control of your financial choices. Small changes can lead to big impact, and I'm going to walk with you every step of the time.

Mostly *C's*:
If money feels overwhelming or confusing right now, *you are not alone*. I'm so proud of you for picking up this book because that means you're ready to make a change. While I can't guarantee it will be easy, I can promise I will guide you with grace, encouragement, and practical steps you can start taking *today*. You're going to gain tools, clarity, and confidence, and I'll be cheering you on the whole way!

Warning Signs You Might Be Financially Strained

- Constantly checking your bank balance but still unsure where your money goes.
- Avoiding opening bills or financial emails.
- Putting off budgeting or tracking spending.
- Making frequent small purchases that add up quickly.
- Using credit cards to cover basics like groceries or gas.
- Living paycheck to paycheck despite a stable income.
- Automatically saying no to anything "extra," even when it's meaningful.
- Regularly overdrawing your account or paying late fees.
- Dreading financial conversations with a partner or loved one.
- Shopping online or in stores as a form of stress relief.

Wherever you are right now—whether you feel ahead of the game or you're just trying to stay afloat—I'm so glad you're here.

Because every baby step you take toward better financial habits will not only change *your* future, it might just change your family's legacy and the lives of others around you.

So, are you ready? **Let's do this together.**

Habit #1

Start with What You Have

Do What You Can, with What You Have, Where You Are

"Go get some more bowls!"

"Grab that bucket!"

"Water is leaking everywhere!"

My mom was hollering, and we kids were running every which way, scrambling to keep the rain from flooding the living room.

"Do we have any more dry towels?"

"Did you check the bedroom window to see if it's leaking too?"

The thin glass windows in our just-moved-into trailer were poorly insulated, so when a thunderstorm rolled in, rain gushed in through the windows.

We gathered buckets, bowls, and towels, but water kept leaking through cracks and crevices, soaking the deep-blue carpet and the worn paneled walls.

There weren't enough of us—even with five kids at the time!—to hold all the buckets and bowls, but we did the best we could. And we chose to make it an adventure, like the previous few months of our lives had been.

I was ten years old, and we had just moved into the trailer that would be our temporary home for the next six months. In order to build a house debt-free, my parents had sold our house to fund the new one, which had meant finding a place for all seven of us to live that wouldn't drain their savings while building. So they got creative and found the solution in that old single-wide, two-bedroom construction trailer.

Now, in case you're not familiar with what a construction trailer is, it's basically a mobile home that's been converted into an office for use on a job site. Ours came with some "special features"—like old, dingy blue carpet, a mouse infestation, no air conditioning or heating, no dryer, no stove or oven, and (depending on the day!) sometimes no water or hot water. Yes, very "special" features.

A few years earlier, my parents had worked hard to pay off our house, and then we'd saved, searched, and planned for a dream they'd had for quite some time: building a house in the country and doing it without any debt.

To make that big, audacious goal a reality, they had to think outside the box. First, they saved up and found land to buy. Then, they cleared and prepped the land for building. Next, they sold our house so they could use the money for all the costs involved with building the new house, and all seven of us moved into that old trailer. It was filthy when it was pulled out of storage, but it was completely free for us to use since the company my dad worked for owned it, and it had been sitting unused in a warehouse for years. All we had to do was get it moved onto our land and in habitable condition again.

We spent hours cleaning, scrubbing, prepping, and de-mousing the trailer. By the time we were ready to move in, it had become a decent little home for us while our new home was being built.

As a bonus, it gave us endless opportunities to learn new skills—like how to cook meals without an oven (we got really adept with the microwave and electric skillet), or how to cool down without air conditioning (we would turn on a fan, place a bowl of ice in front of it, and put our face close so the moving air would hit us and the ice at the same time!).

My parents' willingness to think defy the status quo when it came to their money inspired me and taught me that there's almost always a creative solution if you're willing to look for it. Their example is a huge reason my husband and I later set big, unorthodox goals—like paying cash for our first house and getting him through law school debt-free. Their courage to do things differently shaped so much of who I am today.

They did what they could, with what they had, where they were.

Look at What You Have, Not at What You Don't Have

When it comes to financial health, I believe one of the foundational mindsets for success is to start with what you have, right where you are. We can spend months, years—even decades!—waiting for life to get better, for our situation to change, or for things to finally line up just right so we can move forward financially or make headway with our money goals.

But when we're always looking ahead to what we wish we had or where we wish we were, we can miss out on the opportunities sitting right in front of us.

My parents could have given up on their dream of building a house debt-free because it felt so daunting to figure out how to make it actually work. Instead, they came up with a unique solution for where we could live while building our new house—a solution that was basically free and saved thousands of dollars. Rather than walking away from their vision, they thought unconventionally and made it happen.

The real key to financial progress doesn't start with having more money, a different job, less debt, or moving somewhere cheaper. It begins with shifting your mindset. It's about choosing not to wait for your circumstances to change, but to start right now—today—with what you already have.

When we stop focusing on where we think we should be or where others are, we open the door to start noticing the possibilities right where we are.

My parents not only got creative with what they had by moving us into the construction trailer, but they also saved a lot of money by having my dad take on the role of general contractor for the house we were building—a job he'd never done before. Instead of paying someone else to hire and manage all the different contractors and companies involved in building the house, he did this job himself. While this took a lot of extra time, it saved a significant amount of money.

In addition, my parents became masters at negotiating deals for the materials to build our house, from the lumber to the carpet to the light fixtures. They'd ask for discounts everywhere they shopped, approaching different companies (and even contacting different employees at the same company) until they found someone willing to offer a deal.

They did as much of the work themselves as possible too. At night, after my dad came home from his day job, he and my mom would spend a few hours out at the new house cleaning up after the contractors, painting trim and walls, installing doorknobs, putting up light fixtures, or whatever else they could do. If a job could be done by them and it meant saving money, they were all in.

Creativity truly is one of the greatest gifts you can give your financial future. It can open doors you never expected, help you discover solutions you didn't know existed, and give you the perseverance to keep searching for answers, even when the path feels impossible.

Just today, I received a message from someone who felt hopeless about their finances. "We're stuck," she told me, then listed all the reasons their situation felt impossible.

I tried to encourage her, cheer her on, and share some new ideas they could try. But she wrote back, convinced there was nothing left to do. In her mind, they'd tried everything, and nothing had worked.

I know she's been through a lot and faced many financial setbacks. I know she's tired and discouraged. But here's the hard truth: As soon as you start believing you're stuck, you probably are. Why? Because the moment you decide there's nothing you can do, you begin to lose hope.

What You Believe Changes Everything

I get it. It can truly feel like there's no way out. Life can be challenging, and sometimes it's hard to even see the next step. But please don't let yourself give in to the voice that says, *There's nothing I can do*. Believing you *can* is the very first step toward *real* change.

You've likely heard the saying "Whether you think you can or you think you can't, you're right."[1] Our beliefs set the boundaries for what's possible. When you decide you're stuck, you stop searching for solutions and get caught in a spiral of negativity, focusing on how difficult everything is and how unfair life feels.

I want you to remember this: As long as you're breathing, there is hope. No matter where you are or how many times you've been knocked down, there is almost always *something* you can do. Even if it feels like you've tried everything, keep looking. Keep asking, "What's one small thing I can do right now?" Sometimes, just that question can interrupt the mental spiral and open your heart to new possibilities.

When I catch myself staring down the "stuck" path, I try to pause and gently but firmly say, "Crystal, what's one thing you can do today, no matter how small?"

I remember back when my husband and I were first married, and money was really, really tight. We wanted to stay out of debt, but I had just found out I was pregnant with our first baby and had to quit working because I was so nauseated and tired all day long. I knew I had to find some way to make money—and quickly, as our bank account was going to dwindle very rapidly if I didn't.

What could I do? I didn't have a college degree. I didn't have much experience. But I was motivated—and I let that motivation fuel my determination to find a way.

I had a laptop and internet connection, and during those long days at home when I was so ill with morning-noon-and-night sickness, I lay in bed with the laptop and scoured the internet to find ways to earn money from home that wouldn't cost anything out of pocket.

Those web searches and hours upon hours of trying and experimenting and attempting and failing and learning ultimately led to the journey where I discovered blogging, and eventually it was the catalyst for my starting the blog that now—over twenty years later—is our family's sole source of income!

I had no idea what I was doing, but I chose to do something. To start somewhere. To take the next step. To jump out and try.

Instead of giving into the belief that you can't do anything, ask, "What *can* I do?"

That might look like reaching out to a friend or mentor for ideas to help you lower your budget.

It may mean writing down everything that feels overwhelming. (For me, just getting it out of my head and onto paper makes a difference.)

It could be identifying three things to be grateful for right now.

It might be challenging yourself to make do instead of buying something new.

It could be learning a skill that will save or make you money.

It may be taking on a small side job.

It might even begin with reading a book (like this one) to give you ideas and inspiration for your financial situation.

When you choose to do something—even if it feels microscopic—instead of letting fear paralyze you or giving into the negative belief that you are stuck, it helps you shift from feeling powerless to taking ownership. Believing there are still possibilities you haven't discovered helps you hold onto hope and keeps you searching for solutions.

Start with what you have. Believe that options and answers are out there. Then, proactively search for them.

I watched my parents do this over and over. They started with what they had, got creative, and didn't let obstacles stop them from moving forward. Their persistence and resourcefulness in reaching their financial goals gave them so much more freedom and less stress.

Because of their example, I decided from a young age that I didn't want to have debt—no credit card debt, no mortgage, no student loans. If my parents could work hard, get creative, and find a way to pay off their house and then build a new one debt-free, I wanted to see if I could stand on their shoulders and aim even higher: to never go into debt at all.

Of course, that's easy to say when you're fifteen years old, living at home, and your parents are still covering most of your expenses. It's a whole different story when you're out in the real world on your own.

Our Debt-Free Law School Challenge

Some of you might be thinking that no guy would ever go along with my "no debt" dream—but my husband, Jesse, is no ordinary guy. He's a dreamer too, and he's never been afraid to make decisions that go against the grain or that seem a little crazy (or a lot crazy!) to others.

When he and I married at twenty-two and twenty-one, respectively, we set an audacious goal together: Jesse would go to law school without taking on any debt. We hoped we could stay out of debt after that as well, but starting with no school loans felt like a big first step.

Before our wedding, we spent hours crunching numbers, planning, and researching how we could make law school—and everyday life—work without loans or debt. When I tell people now that Jesse graduated from law school debt-free, most are shocked and assume it's not possible. However, he chose a much less expensive, in-state law school over "prestigious" options, and he earned scholarships, all of which drastically lowered the total cost.

Jesse's journey was also helped by wise planning: After Jesse's mom passed away when he was twelve, his dad invested some of the money Jesse received after her death for future college expenses. Jesse lived at home for most of undergrad (except for one year at a private university in Virginia), so he used only a small portion of those savings. When the time came for law school, we realized we'd have enough to pay cash—if he kept costs down by staying in state and maximizing scholarships. But we'd have to get very creative about how to pay for our living expenses and stretch every dollar.

That's where my parents' example inspired me. I began learning everything I could about saving on groceries. My mom had given me a head start by having me handle menu planning, grocery shopping, and cooking for our family, which had grown to nine when I was a teen and looking for outside-the-box ways to make our dollars go further! I also brainstormed new ways I could bring in extra income.

This is what it truly looks like to live out Habit #1: Start with what you have.

The Drugstore Game

At the beginning of our marriage, since money was so tight and we'd made the commitment to stay out of debt, I decided to treat our budget almost like a game: How little could I spend on groceries and still make sure we ate well? How far could I stretch a bag of chicken? How many free date-night ideas could I come up with? How long could I go without buying any clothes? (For the record, I discovered I could easily go for months without buying anything new or even thrifted.)

I got incredibly creative—so much so that when I share some of what I did on the pages ahead, some of you might think I am a little nuts! As a reminder, I share our story not for you to replicate what we did or to say that our way is the only way or the best way, but just to inspire you to realize that there are usually many outside-the-box options available to try when it comes to finances. Not everything we did back in those days would work now, but I hope this might challenge you to think about ways you could save that you may not have thought of before.

Early on in our marriage, we lived in a tiny basement apartment, and with Jesse gone at work and law school for long hours, I did what I could. I sold items we didn't need on eBay (and then started buying items wholesale to resell on eBay). I worked remotely doing marketing and advertising sales for a homeschool magazine. I wrote articles for online sites that paid a small amount. I resold books. I made a little bit of extra cash every month doing mystery shopping and taking online surveys. I began dabbling in blogging and affiliate marketing. I also spent a lot of time online researching ways to save money.

The internet was a whole different world back in those days. Yes, there was a time when you could only get online on an actual computer, not a phone, and everything was email, websites, and this new thing for college students called Facebook. I spent hours on online message boards and Yahoo! Groups digging for deals.

One of my favorite message boards was Slickdeals. People would post all sorts of tips on scoring deals at local stores and online.

A hot topic on Slickdeals back then was the rewards program at CVS. I'd never even heard of CVS before, as we didn't have them in our town, but I discovered a local drugstore was being bought out by CVS, so I read everything I could about it and decided to try their rewards program.

Here's how it worked: Every week, CVS would advertise five or six items that, if you bought them, you'd get the full amount back in ExtraCare Bucks (ECBs)—a printed receipt that worked like a gift card in-store. The strategy, dubbed "the drugstore game," was to buy those weekly ECB items and then use your ECBs from one week to pay for the next week's deals, rolling them over and over so you rarely paid much cash out of pocket.

If you wanted to get even more from the deals, you'd pair them with manufacturer coupons. For example, if Colgate toothpaste was $2.69 at CVS and you got $2.69 back in ECBs, and you also used a $0.75 off coupon, you'd only pay $1.94 (plus tax) and still get back $2.69 in ECBs—meaning you were essentially "making money" on every tube of toothpaste!

You could maximize your savings even further by stacking these with CVS store coupons. There was a little kiosk at the store that printed coupons every visit when you scanned your CVS card—like $3 off a $15 purchase or $2 off a $10 hygiene purchase. And yes, you could use multiple coupons in a single transaction (we call this "stacking coupons" in the frugal world!).

How I Played the Drugstore Game at CVS

STEP 1 **Buy Weekly Sale Items**
Find items in the ad that offer 100% back in Extra Care Bucks (ECBs).

STEP 2 **Use Coupons**
Stack manufacturer coupons and CVS store coupons for extra savings.

STEP 3 **Pay with ECBs**
(From Previous Week)
Use ECBs from last week to lower your out-of-pocket cost. *(Aim for $1 or less!)*

STEP 4 **Earn New ECBs**
Get new ECBs for this week's qualifying purchase.

STEP 5 **Repeat Next Week**
Add milk, diapers, or essentials.
(Use coupon overage.)

I did a few small test runs at our just-turned-into-a-CVS store, and when the deals actually worked, I went all in. I started spending a few hours each week planning my CVS trips with one goal: to pay as little out of pocket as possible. (You couldn't have a negative total or the deals wouldn't work, so I'd crunch the numbers to get it down to $0.10 or $0.20 out of pocket per transaction.) I often did multiple transactions in one trip, using the ECBs from one order to pay for the next, racking up more ECBs with each purchase.

Yes, I was that "crazy coupon lady" who'd wheel my cart up to the checkout and say, "Ring these three things up first." I'd pay (with ECBs, and maybe a dime), then hand over the items for my next transaction, and say, "Okay, now ring up these next four items." I'd use the ECBs earned from my first transaction to almost fully cover the second transaction and then earn more that I'd use for the third transaction.

You might already be thinking I'm a little kooky, but wait, it gets better. In the early days of the ECB program, there were no limits on the quantity of a single item you could buy and still earn ECBs. So, if Colgate toothpaste was on sale for $2.69 with $2.69 ECBs back, I could buy five or even ten, if the store had them in stock—and get $2.69 ECBs back for each one. To maximize my savings, I'd go dumpster diving in the recycling bin behind the grocery store for newspapers with coupons for $0.75 off one tube of toothpaste. (Don't worry, it was pretty clean, and I figured I was just recycling the coupons myself!)

Here's what a typical trip might look like:

- Buy five tubes of toothpaste at $2.69 each = $13.45
- Add a gallon of milk at $3.19
- Use coupon for a $3 off $15 purchase
- Use five $0.75 off one manufacturer's coupons
- Pay with a $9.80 ECBs earned last week + $0.09 out of pocket
- Earn $13.45 in new ECBs

Then I'd take that $13.45 in ECBs and roll it into the next week's deals. By stacking store coupons, manufacturer coupons, and ECBs, I could often buy $60+ worth of household products and groceries for less than $1 out of pocket—and walk away with $10–$20 in ECBs to use the next time.

I would sometimes go to CVS multiple times a week and repeat this process, so over a few years, I scored thousands of dollars' worth of groceries and household items for under $100 out of pocket. I even found ways to use the overage from coupons and deals to purchase other essentials we needed to buy that week, so we almost never paid for things like diapers, milk, over-the-counter medicine, razors, toothpaste, hair-care products, makeup, and so many other household, hygiene, and personal items during those years.

Note: The drugstore deals aren't quite as amazing as they used to be, but there are still many ways to get hygiene, food, and personal products at rock-bottom prices by pairing coupons and sales with drugstore rebate programs. We share the best drugstore deals weekly on MoneySavingMom.com.

These drugstore deals were a huge blessing to our tiny budget, but the impact didn't stop there! Because I often had more than enough for our family, I was able to give away products to those in our community. Plus, we hosted a few garage sales with friends and sold surplus toothpaste, deodorant, and razors for $0.75–$1 each. People were thrilled with the deals, and that extra money was such a gift to our budget!

Looking back on those lean law school years, I can see how learning to start with what we had provided inspiration and momentum for so many other wins in our lives. It taught me that there's almost always an innovative solution out there. I just have to believe it exists and keep searching, experimenting, and asking others for ideas.

The Freedom to Choose Your Next Steps

Recently I've been reading *Building True Intimacy: Creating a Connection That Stands the Test of Time* by Dan Drake and Joanna and Matthew Raabsmith. In the book, they share a powerful truth that applies to not only relationships, but to every area of life—including our finances:

> No person or situation can make us feel a certain way or do a certain thing. This does not mean that people and situations have zero influence on us. But it does mean being willing to acknowledge that we always have a choice in our responses.[2]

The authors add,

> When we fool ourselves into believing we don't have a choice, we can't be held accountable. The practice of responsibility means that because we don't "have to" do anything, we get to decide whatever it is we do.[3]

That'll preach! The reality is, we do have choices. There are very few situations in life where we don't have some control over our actions—and even when our options for action are limited, we can always choose our attitude.

As I often remind my kids, "I can't always choose my circumstances, but I can choose my response. And my response is my responsibility."

Recognizing our autonomy and ownership over our lives gives us a fresh sense of purpose and motivation. We don't have to go through life as victims of our circumstances. We can choose to start right where we are, use what we have, and make the most of it.

Maybe we won't go as far or as fast as someone else. But believing we're capable of moving forward—even if just one step at a time—is already a huge victory.

Starting with What You Have Is the Foundation for Future Wins

Practicing this habit isn't just about your bank account. It's a mindset that can transform every area of your life—from your career to your calling to your relationships and routines. If you've ever felt stuck, overlooked, or like you don't have enough to move forward, it's often because you are believing the lie that you need *more* to begin: more time, more money, more experience.

But most breakthroughs don't start with abundance. They start with a seed planted or a small idea that grows because someone decided to nurture it. When you begin by taking stock of what God has already placed in your hands, you'll be amazed at how much you already have to work with.

Quick Wins for Your Wallet

Simple, Practical Things You Can Do Right Now to Improve Your Financial Health

- **Check your bank balance today.** Awareness is the first step to financial confidence.
- **Unsubscribe from one promotional email.** Fewer temptations = fewer impulse buys.
- **Cancel one unused subscription.** Even $5 a month adds up to $60 a year.
- **Make a "use what you have" meal plan.** Skip the grocery run and get creative in the kitchen.
- **Transfer $10 to savings.** It's not about the amount; it's about the habit.
- **Return something you don't truly need or love.** Get the refund, not the regret.
- **Say no to one unnecessary purchase.** You're not depriving yourself. You're empowering your future self.
- **Automate a small savings transfer.** Even $1 a day adds up!
- **Do a 10-minute wallet or purse cleanout.** Toss old receipts and find unused gift cards.
- **Delete saved payment info from one shopping site.** Reduce impulse buying.
- **Pack a lunch or snacks for tomorrow.** One skipped takeout = instant savings.
- **Put a sticky note in your wallet with a savings goal.** A visual reminder before spending.
- **Create a "Spending Pause" list.** Wait 48 hours before buying nonessentials.
- **Plan a "no-spend weekend."** Challenge yourself to get creative with free fun.
- **Look for one bill to reduce.** Start with internet, TV, or your phone plan. Call and ask for a discount.
- **Review your last bank statement.** Highlight nonessential spending.
- **Sell one item you don't use.** Facebook Marketplace is your friend.
- **Search your email for "free trial."** Cancel any free trial you signed up for that you forgot to cancel and are now getting charged for.

The Start-Where-You-Are Inventory

To help you begin, I've created the Start-Where-You-Are Inventory. This is a step-by-step process to guide you as you shift from scarcity to sufficiency. It's all about opening your eyes to the resources you already have so you can take intentional, faith-filled action.

Just like I did as a newlywed when I had to quit working after finding out I was pregnant while my husband was in law school, I want to challenge you to consider what you have that could improve your financial situation.

As I mentioned earlier, I had a laptop, an internet connection, Google, email, access to Yahoo! Groups to learn from others, a library card, a few friends who had started online businesses who could give me wise counsel, and I had time—lots and lots of time!

So I started with what I had. I used the laptop and internet connection and Google to research how to make money from home. I made a big list of ideas and then started slowly educating myself on what each one entailed and thinking through which ones were viable for me to do. As I learned more, I emailed people I had connections with or asked people on Yahoo! Groups for advice and information about what had worked for them. In addition, I would go to the library and check out stacks of books on how to start your own business, how to make money, and how to save money.

Then, I began jumping in and trying things. Ultimately, some of the things I tried led me to blogging and affiliate marketing, which have turned out to be the bread and butter of our business today. It's going to look very different for you, but I share this as an example of how you can use what you have and begin with that.

Step 1: What Do I Have in Hand?

Stop and take inventory. What do you already own or have access to that could help you get traction financially—to earn more money to pay down debt, to save more aggressively, or to help you lower your spending.

For example, do you have

- A laptop or smartphone with internet access?
- Craft supplies, baking tools, or a library card?
- Unused gift cards, store credits, or subscriptions?

You could use a laptop or phone with internet access to take a free online course and learn a skill that you could use to earn some side income or to list items you already own to sell and pay off debt. You could also follow frugal websites and gather savings ideas and watch YouTube videos to learn more about budgeting.

If you have craft supplies, you could use them to make products to sell at a local market or online to earn extra income. If you have baking tools, learn how to make your own bread and baked goods to save money—or even to sell to friends and neighbors for extra income.

A library card can unlock all sorts of savings, from free books, ebooks, audiobooks, and DVDs for entertainment and education to free classes or memberships to local attractions. (Check out what your library offers. You may be able to replace some monthly expenditures, such as paying for ebooks or audiobooks or other streaming subscriptions or memberships, with what your library offers for free.)

Use untapped gift cards to reduce grocery or gift expenses this month or sell them online to earn a little cash. Do you need all the subscriptions and memberships you currently pay for?

Could you cancel one or more and redirect that money toward another financial goal?

In the early years of our marriage, we didn't have wiggle room in our budget for eating out. So I got creative. I had heard of this thing called "mystery shopping," where you would get paid to go to restaurants and evaluate their food and service. You would keep track of how long it took from the time you placed your order until your order arrived, whether your server offered you the special, how they greeted you, how often they refilled your water, and so on. The trick was that they couldn't know you were the designated mystery shopper. You had to keep track of all of this information and remember it without attracting any attention to yourself. The companies would then use this real-time feedback to improve their service.

Depending upon the restaurant and how they ran their mystery shopping program, you would usually get two meals free and you would get paid a small amount for your time and effort. This is how we afforded our date nights. It was unconventional, but it worked, and we have so many special memories of our mystery shopping dates, when we got dinner for free and made a little money too!

Step 2: Who Can I Learn From?

Who could you learn from to help impact your financial health and well-being? For instance, do you have a friend who is a pro at budgeting or saving money? Does your library or community center offer free classes on topics like couponing, baking bread, or starting a small business? Are you part of any Facebook groups, forums, or communities where you could ask questions and get feedback to help you become more financially savvy?

Growth doesn't happen in isolation. Who is already doing what you want to do—and doing it well? Make a list of people who are a few steps (or miles) ahead of you. Think of entrepreneurs, mentors, or influencers you follow, people in your community you respect, friends or family who have wisdom in a specific area, or authors or speakers you admire, then reach out and ask a few questions, or just listen to their podcasts, read their books, watch their videos, and soak up what they are doing and teaching.

My mom first learned how to use coupons from a friend in our church named Renee. Not only was Renee an incredible wealth of knowledge and a woman who could easily stretch $5 to buy $30 to $50 worth of groceries, but she was so generous in sharing her wisdom (and her terrific deal finds) with others.

Once my mom learned from her how to use coupons, my mom then started teaching me. Before I got married, my mom made a coupon box for me just as Renee had taught her to make one for herself. This consisted of a shoebox-sized tub with a lid and envelopes that were color coded and alphabetized for different sections of the store and different types of products (dairy, meat, produce, cereal, etc.).

I am so grateful for both Renee and my mom who came before me and laid the foundation for our family to save thousands of dollars on our grocery bill over the years! Little did I know that these skills would one day serve as the foundation for starting a blog that was about saving money and would give me the opportunity to teach millions of people around the globe how to cut their budget.

Step 3: How Much Time Do I Have?

So often, people tell me that they want to save money but they just don't have time. I want to challenge you to look closely at how you are spending your time and see if there are small time leaks you could repurpose (scrolling, binge-watching . . . or maybe even time you're spending worrying about something!).

Could you wake up thirty minutes earlier once a week to write, plan, pray, or work on your dream before the day begins?

Use lunch breaks to watch training videos or send pitch emails? Swap fifteen minutes of scrolling social media for brainstorming business ideas or listening to a helpful podcast?

It is amazing what you can do in fifteen- and thirty-minute blocks of time when you consistently show up and focus on learning, growing, and applying yourself. In fact, one of my books, *The Time-Saving Mom*, was written almost entirely in five- and fifteen-minute segments of time over the course of six months. We had three teens, a toddler, a baby with significant medical complexities and disabilities we were fostering (who we later adopted); I was pregnant; and I was running our business full-time. So my plate was very full. But I had committed to write the book, and so I got creative in finding ways to make it happen.

It wasn't ideal to write a book in tiny snippets of time, but it got done, and with a few rounds of editing, the book ended up being really solid—and it proved to me that you can accomplish big projects (like writing a 55,000-word book!) in small windows of time as long as you show up consistently again and again and again.

Step 4: From Inventory to Action

Now take everything we've talked about:

- What you have in hand
- Who you can learn from
- How much time you have

This is your unique starting point. Now is the time to face your fears and just start, using what you already have.

Look at a dream, goal, or area where you feel stuck. Ask yourself, *What is one small action I can take today using something I already have?*

The power of **Habit #1: Start with what you have** is that it turns excuses into action. No longer can you sit and say, "I'm waiting until I have more money, more time, a better job . . ." or whatever it is that has been holding you back from taking action.

Starting with what you have is the way you rewrite the narrative that you're not ready. You already have enough to do *something*, right where you are.

Small steps, taken consistently, become steady progress. And steady progress leads to lasting change. That's how financial health, and a fulfilling life, are built.

Start where you are. Use what you have. Do what you can.

I hope that going through this exercise inspires you to see that you already have a lot of resources and knowledge at your disposal. Instead of sitting there feeling like the only way your life can change is if your circumstances change, begin with what you have.

Journaling Prompt

Take that first step toward better habits by asking yourself the following four questions and writing down honest answers in a notebook. These questions might sound similar, but I want you to journal whatever comes to mind as you read each question, even if your answers are somewhat the same. This will help you define and process through what your next step could or should be.

As you consider improving your financial health, ask yourself

- What's within my control at this moment?
- What's one thing I can do immediately?
- What's the first step I can handle now?
- What's my most useful next action?

In chapter 2, we'll build on this foundation by helping you clarify your financial goals so you can start making a game plan to work toward them.

10 Simple Ideas to Make Money from Home

Are you looking for a way to bring in extra income? Maybe you want to help make ends meet, save for a special goal, or just add a little breathing room to your budget? If so, there are many income-earning activities to try from the comfort of your own home.

Here are ten tried-and-true ideas (all of which I or my readers on MoneySavingMom.com have personally done) that you can start today:

1. **Sell Unused Items Online**
   Declutter your home and make some cash by selling items you no longer need on Facebook Marketplace, eBay, or Poshmark. Start with kids' clothes, gently used toys, books, and household goods. You'll be amazed how quickly small sales can add up!
2. **Become a Virtual Assistant**
   Small business owners, bloggers, and busy professionals often need help with administrative tasks. If you're organized and reliable, offer your services as a VA. Start by reaching out to local businesses or browsing listings online. (Need help getting started? Visit my store page on MoneySavingMom.com for my Work-From-Home Blueprint course.)
3. **Babysit or Offer Childcare**
   If you love kids, consider babysitting or providing childcare in your home. Even a few hours a week can make a difference for families and for your wallet.
4. **Pet Sit or Dog Walk**
   Animal lovers can earn money by caring for neighbors' pets while they're away, or by offering dog-walking services. Check pet-sitting sites online or let your community know you're available.
5. **Freelance Your Skills**
   Can you write, design, proofread, or manage social media? You could freelance for local churches or shops in your area. Start by

offering your services very affordably while you gain experience, and then slowly raise your rates.

6. **Prep Meals or Bake for Others**
   If you love cooking or baking, make freezer meals, baked goods, or healthy snacks for busy families. Word of mouth and local Facebook groups are great ways to attract customers.
7. **Flip Thrift Store or Garage-Sale Finds**
   Hunt for bargains at thrift stores, at yard sales, or on clearance racks, then resell items online for a profit. Look for brand-name clothing, unique décor, or collectibles. Sometimes all it takes is a little cleaning and good photos!
8. **Host a Parents' Night Out**
   Offer a one-evening babysitting service at your home, providing games, snacks, and fun for kids while parents enjoy a date night. Charge per child and watch the word spread in your community.
9. **Become a Social Media Manager**
   Local businesses often need help with their Facebook or Instagram pages. If you enjoy creating posts and engaging online, pitch your services to small business owners in your community.
10. **Assemble Furniture or Do Minor Repairs**
    Handy with tools? People will pay for help assembling IKEA furniture, hanging shelves, or fixing small household items. Advertise in local Facebook groups or on TaskRabbit.

Habit #2

Decide Your Financial Priorities

Name Your Why and Set Your Compass

I could hardly sleep the night before—I was just *that* excited. This was the day I'd been looking forward to for weeks.

Before the sun had even peeked over the horizon, I was up, dressed, and gathering my supplies to head over to our neighbor's house. Why? Because it was the day of our neighborhood garage sale, and six-year-old me had big plans.

I had convinced my parents to let me set up a lemonade stand. My very own business!

Armed with a little card table, a stack of Dixie cups, and a big pitcher of freshly stirred lemonade, I set up shop and proudly greeted each potential customer who walked by. "Lemonade! Just twenty-five cents a cup!" I'd call out. (And yes, I know that sounds ridiculously cheap, but remember, it was the 1980s, when a quarter for a tiny cup of lemonade wasn't unheard of.)

I doubt that many of the people who purchased were genuinely thirsty, but they kindly supported a young entrepreneur (and many paid more than twenty-five cents and told me to keep the change). By the end of the day, I had earned what felt like a lot of money to my little six-year-old self. I was elated!

One of the very first things I did? I set aside 10 percent of my earnings to bring to church on Sunday and joyfully dropped it into the little plastic church building we used for our Sunday School offering.

Why was I so excited to give? Because generosity had been modeled for me from the time I was little. My parents had shown me that money isn't just something you spend, it's something you work hard for, save intentionally, and use to bless others.

Looking back, I'm so grateful my parents didn't just *talk* about money—they *lived* their values. They had decided before I was born that generosity was a huge priority for them when it came to finances and they worked hard to be in a position to be givers. Their example rubbed off on me, and it inspired me, from a very young age, to be excited to give money as soon as I had it.

Whether we realize it or not, the way our parents or caregivers growing up interacted with money has likely had a profound impact on us—either negative or positive. So to really dive into the topic of financial priorities, I think it's important that we rewind back to childhood and think about how our upbringing has shaped our view of money.

Discovering How We Were Formed

In the last chapter, I shared how my parents built our house debt-free. What I didn't say was that this dream had been years in the making, shaped by generations of intentional living and wise choices.

My mom's parents were some of the most hardworking, generous people I've known. Though my grandma passed away from cancer when I was eleven, her legacy left a lasting impact. She worked outside the home and faithfully taught adult Sunday school for years. She constantly had a project going and was always heading up a committee or an event, even during the many years when she was struggling with significant health issues. Despite her full schedule, she always had time for us, and I have so many special memories of time we spent together in my first decade of life.

My grandpa worked a job he didn't love at the local water station because it provided for his family, but he never stopped dreaming of one day flying a plane. When he retired, he built ultralight airplanes from scratch, taught himself to fly, and flew them for years. At almost ninety-eight years old (as of the writing of this book), his body may be slowing, but his mind and memories are sharp. His stories of growing up during the Great Depression—such as often surviving on salads made from whatever edible plants they could find on the land they lived on—gave me perspective on gratitude and resourcefulness.

My paternal grandparents also blessed me with a rich legacy of financial responsibility. My grandma (who we called "Gammy") was a world-class homemaker who ran her home with steady rhythms and stretched every dollar with creativity. My grandpa (we called him "Pop") was a firm believer in living debt-free and taught my dad that you should never borrow money for anything other than a house. I vividly remember the day Pop and Gammy told us they were building a new home, paid for in cash. That decision, built on years of frugal living, left a deep impression on me.

When my parents got married, they brought those values with them. They bought a tiny, fully furnished home from a relative, fixed it up, and sold it for a profit. By the time I was born, my parents had no debt beyond a mortgage, along with a fierce determination to pay it off quickly.

Even as my dad's income grew, they continued to live on far less than they made, putting the rest toward savings and paying off the mortgage. When I was seven, they paid off their house and then continued to live on much less than they made, saving all they could with the dream of buying land and building a house on it.

There was no internet back then, so they mailed off for a thick house plan catalog. We spent evenings flipping through the pages, circling our favorites. The plan we all loved was too expensive for their cash budget, so we ended up choosing a simpler one—a two-story three-bedroom home with a wraparound porch and an unfinished basement my dad would finish himself down the road.

After a few years of planning and carefully saving, my parents found a plot of twenty-seven acres close to where they lived in Wichita, Kansas. They ended up buying it with cash, and we all set to work getting it ready to build on. We spent many a Saturday out on the property, clearing brush, repairing the outbuildings, and deciding where the house would be built.

Their vision of building a house debt-free carried us through those long and hot days of prepping the land, moving out to the construction trailer, and living without air conditioning for months. We pressed on—scrimping, saving, and working together. Because every sacrifice brought us one step closer to my parents' dream.

Just as the house plans we chose gave our family a clear, tangible vision of what the end result would be, having a financial plan can do the same for you and the future you're building. When you know where you're headed and what matters most to you, you'll be able to make wise, purposeful choices, even when things feel hard or slow or overwhelming.

And that's exactly what we're going to focus on in the next few pages: helping you map out your own vision. We're going to get super practical about identifying your financial priorities and creating a plan that works for *your* life.

I See You

Maybe you've been reading this chapter and thinking, *That's great for her . . . but that's not my story.* There is a very good chance that many of you reading this didn't grow up with parents or grandparents who modeled wise money habits. It's possible you never even had a budget conversation growing up, or the only example you saw was financial tension and survival mode.

If that's you, please hear this: You are not disqualified and you are absolutely *not* alone.

Your past doesn't have to define your future. You get to choose what comes next. And I'm here to walk with you as you take those first, brave steps toward building something new.

As I mentioned in the introduction, before I began writing this book, I conducted an anonymous survey of nearly four thousand women, asking them to share how they relate to money. I asked them to be completely honest in their responses.

Close to half of the participants actually had pretty solid financial upbringings, which I loved to hear! I have a hunch this might be a bit lopsided in that direction compared with the general population because the audience I surveyed were followers of MoneySavingMom.com. And I noticed a theme in the responses that many who had good money habits today credit that to their upbringing and seeing their parents be thoughtful with their finances.

I find this so encouraging because it reminds us that our choices today can deeply impact future generations. Just your reading this book says a lot about your desire to be wise with your money, and I want to remind you that this will make a difference—not only in your personal finances but likely in the lives of those around you too.

That said, there were quite a few respondents who didn't have great examples when it came to money growing up. In fact, over **26 percent** of the women who responded said their parents spent most of their energy just trying to make ends meet and didn't have the capacity to teach them about money.

Another **9.4 percent** said their parents tried to teach them, but it felt like they didn't really know what they were doing.

And **9 percent** shared that money was a completely *taboo* subject in their home. It simply wasn't discussed.

I asked a follow-up question: "Would you like to share more about what it was like growing up and what your parents taught you about money?"

Some of the responses are heartbreaking. But they're important for two reasons:

1. **These women's experiences remind us why learning to manage money matters so much.** The legacy we leave—especially to our children—can be one of intention, quiet clarity, and purpose.
2. **These women's experiences can remind you that you are not the only one.** If you grew up in a household where money was mismanaged or mishandled, I want you to know: You are not alone in experiencing this. And you are not destined to repeat the patterns of your parents. You can forge a new path and build a different future.

Here's what a few women shared regarding what they learned about money in their childhood homes:

> "I heard my parents fighting about a medical bill for me. Later they divorced. I was pretty sure it was my fault. Now I know it had nothing to do with me."

"I remember stealing food to feed my brothers. Money wasn't something we had—let alone something we talked about."

"Money was tight, and spending extra on anything was rarely allowed. Now I struggle to pass up anything that's 'a good deal,' even when I don't need it, because I'm afraid I'll miss my chance."

"I started working at 14 to help pay bills."

"In my mom's family, money was used to buy affection and control. When she inherited money, she spent impulsively on high-end things—and she never learned to manage it wisely."

"It was always stressful. My parents made good money, but lived beyond their means. They encouraged us to do better, but never taught us how."

If you read those words and found yourself nodding, or if they stirred something deep in your heart, know this:

Your financial past impacts your financial future, but it doesn't have to dictate it.

Stop and read that again because it's so important.

You do *not* have to repeat the patterns you were shown.

You do *not* have to carry the weight of your parents' mistakes.

You can choose a new path. You can build something different—something *better*. And I'm here to walk with you as you do.

Let's Take a Look Back

I want to take a few minutes to consider how your parent(s) or caregiver(s) related to money and how that may have shaped you, even unknowingly.

Often, much of how we think about money today is deeply connected to what was modeled for us in childhood. Whether your parents talked openly about money or avoided it altogether, whether they modeled wise habits or struggled constantly to make ends meet . . . their relationship with money likely had a big impact on yours.

When you can carve out some quiet time, pull out a journal and reflect honestly on the questions below. There are no right or wrong answers. This is just a chance to notice, name, and better understand your starting point.

Journaling Prompts

1. **What messages did I hear about money growing up?**
    - Was money talked about regularly or rarely mentioned?
    - Did it feel like there was never enough? Just enough? Always extra?
    - Were those conversations tense, peaceful, secretive, or open?
2. **How did my parent(s) or caregiver(s) typically spend money?**
    - Were they savers or spenders?
    - Did they budget carefully or spend impulsively?
    - Did they use money to reward, control, express love, or relieve stress?
3. **What did I learn (explicitly or implicitly) about saving?**
    - Was saving encouraged?
    - Did I see anyone saving for long-term goals?
    - Was saving viewed as wise or as a restriction?
4. **What did I learn about giving?**
    - Was generosity a value I saw lived out?

- Did my parent(s) or caregiver(s) give to church, a charity, or others in need?
- Did they talk about why giving matters?

5. **What did I learn about debt?**
   - Was debt normal and expected?
   - Was it avoided at all costs?
   - Did I see credit cards or loans used regularly?
6. **Was money used as a means of control in our home or leveraged to buy peace?**
   - Were there arguments about money?
   - If you were raised by two parents/caregivers, did they work as a team financially, or did one person handle it all?
   - Was there pressure or shame attached to financial decisions?
7. **How did these experiences affect the way I think about money today?**
   - Do I feel confident managing money, or overwhelmed?
   - Am I mimicking what I saw, or reacting against it?
   - Have I intentionally chosen my money habits, or just inherited them?

As you reflect, remember: This isn't about blaming or shaming anyone. It's about *understanding*, so you can grow from it.

Some of you may look back and realize you were handed a beautiful foundation of wisdom and intentionality. If so, what a gift! Celebrate that and carry it forward.

But for others, this exercise might stir up hard memories or painful patterns. If that's you, please know: You are not stuck. You are not forever destined to follow in your parents' footsteps. Instead, let this awareness motivate you to make changes that will not only deeply impact your future, but also could leave a legacy for those who follow after you.

How to Begin Changing Old Patterns Once You Identify Them

Recently I posed this question on Instagram to those who *don't* currently use a budget: **"Would you be willing to share anonymously and honestly with me why you don't use a budget?"**

I expected to hear some of the usual responses, and sure enough, many people said things like

- "I don't know how to set one up."
- "I don't think I make enough money to need a budget."
- "My spouse doesn't want to have a budget."

If you read those and thought, *That's me!* Please know you're in good company. And don't worry, we're going to tackle every one of those objections together in the coming chapters. I've got practical tools to help you get started, even if budgeting feels impossible right now.

But what surprised me most? The *deeper* responses.

Over and over again, people shared a much more vulnerable reason for avoiding a budget:

"I'm scared to look at the numbers."

They weren't just unsure how to create a plan; they were terrified of what that plan might reveal.

Many said that seeing the actual numbers felt too overwhelming, too heavy, too shameful. So instead, they chose to stay in the dark . . . because *not knowing* felt safer than facing the truth.

Friend, I get it. Pretending everything's fine can feel like a way to cope. But here's the truth: *You can't change what you won't confront.*

If you never take the time to face where you are financially, you can't move in a better direction. In fact, there's a good chance you'll stay stuck—or even slip further behind—simply because you're afraid to open up your bank app and see where you are spending money or how much money you have in your account.

You have two choices:

1. You can keep your head in the sand. Keep avoiding the truth. Keep carrying around that low-level dread that *maybe* the numbers are worse than you think.
2. **Or** . . . You can choose courage. You can take a deep breath, face the reality of where you are, and start building a plan to move forward, one small step at a time.

Because you can't experience financial health if you aren't willing to first assess where your finances are in the first place.

Imagine you're in an unfamiliar room that's pitch black. You're afraid to move because you don't know what's around you, and everything feels scary. But the second you flip on the light, it's just a room. Maybe messy. Maybe crowded. But not dangerous. And now you can navigate it.

It's the same with your finances. If you stay in the dark with the lights off, you have no idea where you are, and it can feel overwhelming and dangerous, but turning on the light (getting honest and actually reviewing where you are financially) gives you power. What felt terrifying in the dark becomes manageable in the light.

And it can lead to freedom because you are no longer living in fear. You can see and you are empowered to take the next step.

Notice the Negative and Replace It with Truth

If you have spent years trapped in financial struggles, feeling as though you can never break free, I want to give you some

Healthy Money Mindset Mantras

Have you ever swiped your card to boost your mood, felt a wave of panic when an unexpected bill popped up, or avoided checking your bank account out of shame?

So many of our money habits aren't really about money at all. They're often quiet echoes of what we saw, heard, and felt growing up. Without even realizing it, we carry around old beliefs about money like invisible baggage—sometimes helping us, but often holding us back.

Ask yourself: *Am I trying to soothe something deeper every time I spend?*

One of my friends recently did a thirty-day spending fast and realized she wasn't buying things because she needed them. She was trying to fill a deeper need—using spending as comfort whenever she felt sad or stressed.

Sometimes, we spend to fill a void from a childhood that felt uncertain or lacking. Other times, we hold onto every penny because deep down, we're afraid everything could fall apart just like it did once before.

Your patterns with money today might be your younger self trying to feel safe. But you are not stuck in those old stories. You can learn, you can grow, and you can change. You can break the cycle and build a new legacy—one careful choice at a time.

practical encouragement for the journey. In the last chapter, I had you take inventory of what you already have to work with to help you start moving toward financial health.

In this chapter, we've spent some time looking back at our financial foundation to take stock of what unhealthy patterns and habits and baggage we might need to let go of so we can move forward in freedom.

If you don't know where to begin, start by paying attention to how you speak to yourself, whether out loud, to others, or just the thoughts you allow yourself to think about yourself.

You body and brain internalize negative beliefs and can then act on them or be held back by them. Start noticing and naming these negative beliefs and replacing them with positive truths. (You can use the Start-Where-You-Are Inventory from the last chapter to remind you of all the resources you have at your disposal to help you move forward.)

For instance:

Instead of: "My family has always been terrible with money, and that was handed down to me."
Try: "I am capable of reversing old patterns in my family's financial history."

Instead of: "I'm terrible with money."
Try: "I learned to cope with stress by spending. That helped me survive, but now I'm ready to try something new."

Instead of: "I can't stick to a budget."
Try: "I've never been taught how to create a realistic budget that works for me. Now I'm learning."

Instead of: "I always mess things up with money."
Try: "I've made choices out of fear or survival. Now I want to make choices from a place of wisdom and peace."

Instead of: "I'm just not disciplined enough."
Try: "I've struggled with consistency, but I'm learning to build habits that support the life I want."

Instead of: "I don't know what I'm doing."
Try: "I'm still learning, and that's okay. Every expert once felt uncertain too."

Take it one step further by writing a simple money truth you can repeat when old thought patterns try to creep in. This can be so helpful in encouraging you to replace negative belief patterns with new ones that will serve you better.

Here are some examples:

- "I can make wise choices with money."
- "I don't need to spend money to feel loved or worthy."
- "Money is a tool I can use with intention and clarity."

So often, we try to move forward and create new habits and patterns without digging up the root of why we may have dysfunctional beliefs and mindsets that are holding us back. As I shared earlier in the book, I believe financial health is the quiet confidence and calm that comes from managing your money with intention, seeing money as a tool to bring freedom, not fear, and to serve your life instead of running it.

If we have layer upon layer of deep-seated negative beliefs, dysfunctional mindsets, and unhelpful patterns, it's going to be really tough to move forward with purpose and confidence or to have the fortitude to make wise, intentional choices in our money management. That's why this honest look back matters so much, as it's the foundation for choosing something new.

But here's the good news: Once you've identified what's been holding you back and started the healing work, you get to turn the page. You get to decide what your next chapter looks like.

How to Decide Your Financial Priorities

Now that we've looked back and have processed how to have healthier viewpoints and mindsets, it's time to look forward and decide your financial priorities for today and the future.

This is where the fun and freedom begin! Instead of living on autopilot or letting your money habits be determined by your past, you get to chart a course that aligns with your deepest values, your hopes, and your dreams.

In this section, I'm going to walk you through the reasons your financial priorities matter and help you spell out those priorities so they can serve as a compass for your decision-making and your spending. In addition, this will lay a solid foundation for us to build on in the upcoming chapters.

Why Priorities Matter

Let's pause for a second. Maybe you've never sat down to actually name your financial priorities before. Or maybe you have, but life has changed since you did. Maybe kids came along, jobs shifted, or you simply lost sight of those goals in the busyness of everyday life.

Here's what I know: When you get clear on what matters most, it gives you the ability to say yes and no with purpose. You can tune out the noise and comparison. You're not just saving money for the sake of saving or hustling to pay off debt with no real end in mind. You're living out a mission. You know where you're headed. You know why. And you have a plan to get there. That's what we're going to walk through in the following pages.

My parents are the best example of this. When they decided, before I was born, to pay off their mortgage and someday build a house in the country with cash, they did so because generosity and hospitality were core values for them. They wanted the

What Are Basic Financial Necessities?

As we talk about necessities and needs versus wants, I think it's important to define our terms so we are on the same page. Basic financial necessities are the foundational elements of a healthy financial life. These are the essential areas where your money must go first to cover your needs, protect your well-being, and prepare for the future.

They are the things you need to stay alive, have a job, and function in society. Here's a breakdown of what I consider basic financial necessities:

1. Housing
   - Rent or mortgage
   - Property taxes
   - Home insurance
   - Utilities (electricity, water, gas, trash)
2. Food
   - Groceries
   - Basic household supplies (toilet paper, cleaning products)
3. Transportation
   - Vehicle (if applicable)
   - Fuel
   - Insurance
   - Maintenance and repairs
   - Public transportation costs (bus, train, ride-share)
4. Health and Insurance
   - Health insurance premiums
   - Out-of-pocket medical expenses
   - Dental/vision care
   - Prescription medications
5. Minimum Debt Payments (if applicable)
   - Credit cards
   - Student loans
   - Personal loans
   - (Always make at least the minimums to avoid fees and damage to your credit.)

6. Communication and Connectivity
    - Cell phone bill
    - Internet service
    - (Especially important if you work from home or have school-age children.)
7. Basic Work/School Needs
    - Work clothes
    - Childcare (if needed to earn an income)
    - School supplies or fees

freedom to give and to host people—without the burden of being tied down by debt.

Their example impacted me so much that it shaped my own family's journey. My husband and I set audacious goals because we saw firsthand the peace and purpose that comes from aligning your money with your values. I'll be sharing our financial priorities in a later chapter, but I want to remind you that what our priorities look like will be different from your priorities.

Your Step-by-Step Plan for Setting Financial Priorities

Let's make this super practical. Here's exactly how to uncover and live out your unique financial priorities:

1. **Start with a Vision of Your Priorities**
   So often we can focus on what we don't want or what we've done wrong instead of defining what it is that we do want. Stop and ask yourself
    - What would my life look like if money wasn't the thing holding me back?
    - What do I wish my financial priorities were?
    - What experiences do I hope to be able to give my family?

- Where/how would I love to be able to give generously?
- What financial legacy do I want to leave people in my family when I'm gone? (This could be monetary or it could be making sure we are modeling wise financial practices and money management and handing those down to those around us in our lifetime.)

Write down every thought, both big and small, without second-guessing or psychoanalyzing yourself. Just write down whatever comes to mind.

One thing that helps me to prioritize better is asking myself, "What will matter most twenty-five years from now?" This brings a clearer perspective and better decision-making in the day-to-day.

2. **Name Your Why**

For each question answered above, ask yourself, *Why does this matter to me? Why do I want to prioritize this?* Maybe it's more stability for your kids, creating a bank of family memories and experiences together, the ability to make a difference in the world, freedom from financial tension and strain on your relationships, or simply having more options. Knowing your why will give you grit and motivation on the hard days.

3. **Get Specific**

Now narrow your list to your top three to five priorities. Be honest about what truly excites you, even if it's different from what you feel most people in your life are choosing or prioritizing.

Examples could be

- Paying off all debt
- Giving generously to causes you believe in
- Paying cash for a new-to-you vehicle
- Funding college for your kids, or a niece or nephew

- Meeting needs you see in your community
- Quitting your job to stay home with your kids
- Building an emergency fund
- Creating the means to travel or make memories as a family
- Having the freedom to help other families facing financial challenges

4. **Rank and Reality Check**
   Put your priorities in order. Which one comes first? Which one can wait? Ask: If you had a thousand dollars extra this month, where would you want it to go? That's a clue to what matters most to you right now.
5. **Involve Your People**
   If you're married, make sure you go through this exercise together. Talk with your spouse and see where your lists match (and where they don't). If you're single, share your list with a trusted friend or mentor. Invite feedback, but remember, your list should reflect *your* core values.
6. **Align Your Money with Your Mission**
   This is where the rubber meets the road. Pull out your bank statements, credit card statements, recorded mobile purchases, and any record of cash purchases and look at your last three months of spending. Does it match up with the priorities you named in steps 1 and 2? If not, what's one small adjustment you can make this month to move closer?
   - Maybe it's setting up an automatic transfer from your checking account to savings.
   - Maybe it's choosing a lower-cost family outing so you can give more.
   - Maybe it's saying no to a purchase because your goal matters more.

7. **Build Flexibility and Celebrate Progress**

   Priorities will change as your life changes, and that's not a bad thing! Review and update your list every year or when you hit a big milestone. Is there anything that needs to be adjusted? Consider whether your goals or family or personal priorities have changed at all.

Real-Life Example: Our Family and Business Priorities

Just to give you a peek behind the curtain, here are the priorities that have guided our family and business decisions over the years.

Family Priorities:

1. Giving generously
2. Living debt-free
3. Prioritizing our kids' education (For us, this has meant investing in private schools, classical schools, and homeschooling.)
4. Making memories as a family (locally as well as traveling)
5. Having a six-month emergency fund

   The first four were set from the very start—even when our budget was razor thin. As our income grew, we added an emergency fund and eventually allowed for more flexibility and fun.

Business Priorities:

1. Tithing/giving from our gross income
2. Operating debt-free
3. Caring well for our team
4. Emergency fund for business ups and downs
5. Savings for growth and big opportunities

We started simple: Give and don't borrow. As my blog and online business grew, we built up savings and prioritized our team. Today, we aim to have at least six to nine months of expenses saved for lean times, because online business is unpredictable!

Your Priorities Become Your Compass

When I look back at six-year-old Crystal, who gave a tenth of her lemonade earnings as a Sunday school offering, I can see that my attitudes toward money were being formed at that young age. And that's true of you too.

Whether our caregivers were modeling tithing, saving, and spending or not, we pick up attitudes about money early on. And as we pause to notice whether those attitudes and habits are serving us *today*, we can choose to be intentional about naming the priorities that matter most to us.

How you steward your lemonade money is up to you! But just remember: The priorities you choose will become your compass. Make sure that they help you say yes to what brings calmness and purpose, and no to what's just noise or comparison. Be sure they give you clarity and courage to keep going, even when it's tough.

You get to decide what your financial future looks like—and that decision starts today!

Journaling Prompt

Think of what limiting or negative beliefs you've had around money. Write these down. Then, come up with a positive shift to begin telling yourself to replace the negative beliefs. I've listed some examples to get you started.

Replace Limiting Beliefs with Empowering Mindset Shifts

Instead of . . .	Try This Empowering Shift . . .
"I can't do that."	"What can I do with what I already have?"
"That will never work."	"Is there something I could make work in this situation, even if it looks different than I expected?"
"Our situation is never going to improve."	"What is one small thing I can do today to move toward where I want to be in six months?"
"This is so hard."	"What can I be grateful for where I'm at right now?"
"I don't have enough."	"What do I already have that I've been overlooking?"
"I'm stuck."	"There is always something I can try or learn from this moment."
"I need more time/money/experience."	"How can I get creative with the time, money, and experience I do have?"
"Nothing I do makes a difference."	"Small, consistent steps lead to big change over time."
"I don't know where to start."	"What's one thing I already know how to do that could help me take the next step?"
"Someone else could do this better."	"My unique starting point is a strength, not a setback."

Habit #3

Predetermine Your Spending

Set Up a Money Plan (aka Budget) in Under an Hour

I still remember the way my heart pounded as the nurse called my name and I followed her to the exam room. I felt anxious, exposed, and honestly, a little embarrassed. For months, I'd been quietly battling a health issue, something that had been weighing heavily on me, physically and emotionally.

This doctor visit was years after the hospitalization that I shared about earlier in the book, but it took me back to some of the same fears I'd felt then.

I hadn't told anyone about the issue except my husband. And even when doing that, I kept minimizing it, hoping it would somehow resolve itself. But it didn't. So after lots of inner pep talks and prayers, I finally picked up the phone and scheduled the appointment.

Now here I was, hands clammy and cheeks flushed, sitting in the chilly exam room, preparing to say out loud the things I'd been trying so hard to ignore. The nurse was gentle and kind. She typed as I haltingly shared my symptoms and concerns, then she told me the doctor would be in shortly.

What happened next completely surprised me.

The doctor didn't come in and jump straight into an exam or start rattling off a list of clinical questions. Instead, she pulled up a chair, looked me in the eyes, and said, "Tell me about what's going on."

So I did. I let it all spill out—the fears, the confusion, the helplessness I'd felt. She listened intently with genuine care.

When I finished, she simply looked at me with kindness and said words I'll never forget: "You are in the right place. I'm going to help you. And it's going to get better."

I felt like ugly crying right there in the sterile exam room.

Nothing had changed yet. But everything felt different. Because I wasn't carrying it all alone anymore. I had someone in my corner. Someone who had seen many patients like me before, someone who had experience and training and years of practice helping people like me, and someone who was going to give me a treatment plan, believing things could and would change in a positive way for me.

I share that story because I think that's exactly the way so many women feel about their finances. Afraid. Overwhelmed. Ashamed. They feel they've tried everything and still can't quite figure it out. They feel no one would understand. And they are scared to voice their fears and concerns.

When I asked those four thousand women in the anonymous survey to share their money struggles, I wanted to know what kept them up at night and where they felt stuck.

Here are the top ten money fears that came up again and again in the survey responses. As you read through the list, mentally put a checkmark by any that hit close to home or sound familiar.

Top 10 Most Common Money Fears of Women

1. **Living Paycheck to Paycheck**
   The most common fear: *What if the money runs out?* Many women feel they're just barely getting by. They feel always behind, never able to catch up or get ahead.
2. **Unexpected Expenses**
   What if something happens that I didn't plan for? From car repairs to medical bills, the unpredictability of life is a constant worry, even for those with savings.
3. **Medical Costs**
   Healthcare feels overwhelming and expensive. Whether it's chronic illness, high deductibles, or fear of future medical needs, this is a deeply emotional and financial stressor.
4. **Debt**
   Credit cards, student loans, and medical debt often carry shame and a sense of being stuck. A number of women expressed feeling like they're drowning, with no rescue in sight.
5. **Retirement Challenges**
   What happens when I can't work anymore? Whether they started late or feel unprepared, many survey responses were about worrying that they would about outlive their money.
6. **Rising Costs**
   Groceries, gas, insurance—it can seem like the price of everything keeps going up. Repeatedly, I heard women respond that they feel they're working harder than ever yet have less to show for it.

7. **Housing Insecurity**
   Whether renting or owning, rising costs and surprise repairs leave many wondering, *Can I even afford to stay here?*
8. **Income Instability**
   Especially for those with variable income or a single income source, fear of a job loss, a pay cut, or a reduction in hours is always lingering.
9. **Not Having Financial Confidence**
   I feel behind and don't even know where to start. Budgeting, saving, investing . . . all of it can feel overwhelming, and many shared that they wish someone had just taught them the basics.
10. **Relationship Struggles Around Money**
   Money is one of the biggest sources of tension in relationships. Conflicting values, secrecy, or fears about being left unprepared weigh heavily on many women.

If any of these sound familiar, know that there are so many who feel the same way. However, I want you to experience the same sort of relief I felt when I was in that exam room with the doctor as you read what I wish I could say face-to-face to you: ***You are in the right place. I'm going to help you. It's going to get better.***

I've spent almost two and a half decades learning, developing, practicing, and teaching others the principles and habits I'm sharing with you in this book. After helping hundreds of thousands of families save money and live with more intention through my blog, podcast, books, and digital products, I believe without a doubt that this can work for you too!

You don't have to carry these fears by yourself anymore. I'm here to walk alongside you, guide you step by step, and cheer you on as you move from fear to freedom. It won't always be easy, but I believe in you and I know change is possible.

Let's Talk About the Elephant in the Room

Now we are going to slowly dip our toe into waters that may feel precarious, scary, volatile, or just plain yucky to you. Because yes, we're going to talk about budgeting.

However, if the very word *budget* conjures up all sorts of negative emotions for you, let's replace it with the phrase *money plan*. Because that's what it is.

And if even the thought of having a plan for your money feels a little terrifying or strangling, let me gently offer a new perspective: **What if a budget (aka money plan) isn't a burden, but a gift?** What if it's not about saying *no* to everything, but about saying *yes* to what matters most?

How would it feel to be in a position not only to define what matters most but then also be able to say yes, to follow through and do that thing?

Maybe you are passionate about traveling as a family. What if budgeting allowed you to do that?

Perhaps you have a dream to start a business. What if budgeting allowed you to do that?

Or, you might long to serve and help a specific cause, ministry, or nonprofit. What if a budget allowed you to give generously to an organization or support a cause you wholeheartedly believe in?

A good budget isn't about restriction; it's about intention. It helps you to spend, save, give, and enjoy life with clarity and purpose. It gives you the freedom to buy that coffee or take that trip or write that check to a charity or start that remodeling project *without guilt or fear of the future*—because you planned for it.

A budget is the reason our family can plan for joy-filled things like date nights, vacations, and birthday gifts, and even pay for spontaneous splurges. It is a true asset to our home and our lives, not something that brings shame, stress, and stifling.

When you begin to view a budget as a grace-filled, permission-giving plan for your money, you can see how it's one of the kindest things you can give yourself and your family.

Budgeting doesn't have to feel like punishment. It can feel like peace.

In the pages that follow, I'm going to walk you through—step by simple step—how to set up a plan for your money that

Not a Fan of the Word *Budget*? Try This Instead

If the word *budget* feels restrictive to you, don't let that deter you. Sometimes, just changing how we talk about money can change how we feel about it. Try choosing a term that feels more inviting, one that fits your mindset and goals:

Spending plan—emphasizes thoughtful use of money, not limitation
Money plan—simple and approachable
Financial road map—suggests guidance and direction
Cash-flow plan—sounds more businesslike or strategic
Resource plan—highlights stewardship, useful for values-based personalities
Money map—visual and journey-oriented
Intentional spending guide—underscores choice and purpose
Personal finance plan—broader, less emotionally charged
Values-based spending—ties choices to what matters most

All these terms are still about making your money work for you—just with language that might feel more motivating than overwhelming!

brings clarity, calm, and alignment with your values. But first, I want to let you in on a little secret.

Why I Was Scared to Talk About Budgeting

For years, I believed I wasn't smart enough to teach budgeting, let alone talk about it publicly.

Now here's the ironic part: My husband and I have lived on a budget our entire marriage. That's almost twenty-four years of real-life, hands-on experience! We've discovered the joy and freedom that comes from living within our means. I've built a platform centered on saving money, stewarding resources, and making thoughtful financial choices.

But when it came to teaching *how* to budget? I completely avoided it.

I stuck with the "safe" topics like how to cut grocery costs, stretch your dollars, earn extra income. Those felt doable. Comfortable. Familiar.

I was afraid that teaching people about budgeting would open me up to questions I couldn't answer. *What if I got it wrong? What if I looked foolish or was exposed as a fraud?*

At the root of it? Math.

Math has always been a struggle for me. I barely passed my required classes in high school, didn't go to college, and I've joked that I tap out somewhere around fifth-grade math. Algebra and geometry? They feel like foreign languages. With anything beyond "grocery math," I felt way out of my depth.

For a long time, I steered clear of talking about budgeting. But a few years ago, I felt a quiet nudge in my heart. A pull to stop hiding behind fear and start speaking up about *real* budgeting—not just the numbers, but the heart behind them.

And the moment I gave that idea space to breathe, the doubts showed up:

Who do you think you are?

You're not smart enough.

Stay in your lane.

But I've learned that growth doesn't happen in the safe zone.

So I got brave. I began answering more budgeting questions on my Instagram account and blog posts, including the uncomfortable ones. I studied, practiced, and slowly started sharing more. I launched a twelve-week budgeting series on Instagram. I began considering the idea of writing this book. I even started creating digital products to teach budgeting to both adults and teens.

Each time I stepped forward, the insecurities tried to pull me back. But each time I pushed on, it got a little easier. And I got a little braver.

Still, I knew I needed to face this limiting belief head on. So, during a mastermind meeting with some incredibly wise women before I started writing this book, I stood up and asked, "How do I overcome the belief that I'm not smart enough to teach budgeting?"

One woman raised her hand and said something that stopped me in my tracks:

"You don't have to be good at math to be good at budgeting."

Wait . . . what?

That had *never* occurred to me. I had always equated budgeting with math.

Then another woman added, **"Budgeting isn't about math; it's about prioritization. It's about aligning your spending with your values."**

That truth hit me deep. Because *that*—helping people live in line with their values—is one of my greatest strengths.

All along, I had been focused on what I *wasn't* good at instead of seeing how budgeting actually leverages what I *am* good at: simplifying, planning, creating systems, and helping others make life-giving choices.

So here I am, fears, insecurities, multiple misgivings, and all, showing up to guide you in creating a spending plan that reflects what matters most to *you*.

Not because I'm a math whiz or a spreadsheet queen (full disclosure: I avoid spreadsheets if at all possible!) or because I have well-respected financial degrees.

No, it's because I've *lived* this. I've seen the transformation that intentional money habits can bring. And I believe that the practice of consistent habits won't just change your finances, it will also positively impact your relationship dynamics and your peace of mind!

The Power of Planning for Your Money with a Budget

Having a money plan **puts you in the driver's seat.** Instead of wondering where your money went, you get to *tell* it where to go, as I stated in the "Why This Works" section earlier. A plan gives you clarity, purpose, and control. There's no more guesswork or end-of-the-month surprises.

It simplifies decision-making. When you're unsure whether to spend on something, your budget becomes a built-in guide. It removes guilt and second-guessing and replaces them with confidence.

It gives you permission to enjoy your money. One of my favorite parts of our budget is the "fun money" category. It's a guilt-free way to spend on things that bring you fulfillment and life, such as coffee with a friend, a spur-of-the-moment date with a child, or buying something special without throwing your finances off track.

It leads to long-term success. A budget is a road map to your goals. Whether those goals are paying off debt, saving for a home, giving generously, or simply feeling less financial strain, a budget helps you get there step by step.

If you're married, it brings unity in your marriage. When you sit down and plan your money together, you create space for better communication, shared goals, and teamwork. It might feel uncomfortable at first, but it can actually draw you closer together and strengthen your relationship.

Looking back over our almost twenty-four years of marriage, budgeting has been one of the most life-changing decisions we've made. It hasn't always been easy or perfect, but it has brought joy and freedom we wouldn't trade for anything.

So if the word *budget* feels scary or heavy, that's okay. Call it a spending plan. Call it a peace plan. Call it whatever you want. What matters is that you have a plan.

Because when you do? You create space that yields less stress, more tranquility, and a future full of possibility.

Little by little, that mindset shift changes everything. And that change? It can ripple through your home, your habits, your future—and even through generations to come. Like we talked about in the last chapter, our mindsets get passed down to our children and their children, and their children's children, as well as anyone else watching.

How to Set Up a Budget (Even If You're a Total Beginner)

If you've never created a budget before, don't worry. I'm going to guide you through the process in plain language and in under an hour. Grab a cup of coffee or tea, and let's do this together.

Step 1: Prepare Your Tools (10 Minutes)

Before you begin, gather these items:

- A pen and the budget worksheets (go to MoneySavingMom.com/budgetworksheets for a free downloadable worksheet) or a blank sheet of paper
- Your pay stubs, bank statements, and credit card statements from the past three months
- A calculator

That's it! No complicated spreadsheets or apps required.

Now take a deep breath. I know this part can feel a little scary, especially if looking at your financial reality makes you nervous. But **avoiding your numbers won't make anything better.**

Looking at them honestly is the first step to freedom. And you might even be surprised to see that things are not as bad as you think. Or, if they are, creating a plan will help you feel more empowered to change them.

Step 2: Pinpoint Your Income (10 Minutes)

In order to budget, you need to know how much money you have to work with.

Here's how to figure that out:

1. **List all your income sources**: your job, side gigs, rental income, freelance work, etc. Be conservative. *Only count what you consistently bring in each month.*
2. **Calculate your monthly income.** If you're paid weekly or biweekly, take your total annual income and divide by twelve to get your average monthly income. For irregular income, estimate based on your lowest consistent month.

Example:

Tricia makes $2,600 each month after taxes from her retail job and earns $500 a month from her furniture-flipping side gig.

After setting aside 20 percent for taxes on her side income, that leaves her $400 per month in side income. Her total monthly income = $3,000.

Step 3: Predetermine Your Spending (20 Minutes)

This is where the magic starts. Instead of tracking what's already been spent, you're going to tell your money where to go *before* it leaves your account.

Think of it like labeling every dollar. You're not reacting; you're proactively choosing how to use your income in alignment with your priorities. (Look at the financial priorities list you created in chapter 2 and use it as inspiration for this!)

Start by breaking your expenses into two categories:

Fixed Expenses

These are bills that stay fairly consistent each month. Think things like

- Giving/tithe
- Rent or mortgage
- Property taxes
- Utilities
- Insurance
- Cell phone
- Loan payments
- Tuition/childcare
- Subscriptions (streaming, security system, etc.)

List each one, then total the amount. This gives you a clear picture of your nonnegotiables.

Variable Expenses

These can change from month to month and are typically more within your control. They include

- Groceries
- Gas
- Dining out
- Entertainment
- Clothing
- Gifts
- Miscellaneous

Again, list each one and assign a realistic amount. Look at past months' spending if you're unsure. Be honest! You're only hurting yourself by underestimating.

Now, add your fixed and variable expenses together. Then subtract that number from your monthly income.

Example: Tricia's Fixed Expenses (These are consistent month-to-month.)

Category	Amount
Rent	$1,000
Utilities	$150
Insurance (car + renter's)	$120
Cell phone	$60
Car payment	$250
Subscriptions (streaming, security, etc.)	$40
Total Fixed:	**$1,620**

Example: Tricia's Variable Expenses (These can change month-to-month.)

Category	Budgeted Amount
Groceries	$300
Gas/Transportation	$150
Dining Out	$100
Entertainment	$60
Clothing	$50
Gifts	$30
Miscellaneous	$40
Total Variable:	**$730**

Add Fixed + Variable Expenses:
$1,620 (Fixed) + $730 (Variable) = **$2,350**

What's Left?

- Total Income: $3,000
- Total Spending: $2,350
- **Remaining: $650**

If you have money left after covering your essentials, that is amazing, and you can decide how you want to prioritize that (preferably to save for taxes, one-time expenses, or toward a savings goal—more on that later). If you found that you are spending more than you are making right now, don't feel discouraged. I'm going to give you a lot of tools and strategies in the rest of the book to help you lower your expenses.

It's okay if the numbers aren't where you want them to be right now. The goal isn't perfection; it's progress. We'll keep working through the numbers together as we move through this book. Your current situation is just a starting point, not the end of the story. Don't give up. Keep going. Small steps forward move you in the right direction.

Step 4: Prioritize Your Paycheck

Your paycheck can only stretch so far, so how you prioritize it matters. It's easy for money to disappear without a plan, leaving you wondering where it all went. In this section, we'll take a clear-eyed look at how to maximize the mileage of your money, making sure the most important needs are met first, while still leaving space for what matters to you. Whether your income is steady or unpredictable, the goal is the same: Make your money work for you, not the other way around.

As you calculate where your dollars are going each month, the goal is to give *every* dollar a purpose.

If your expenses are higher than your income, don't panic. This is an opportunity to look at what can be trimmed or cut for now. And if cutting isn't enough, it may be time to explore simple ways to increase your income, even temporarily. (Revisit chapter 2 for ideas of ways to increase your income and see the upcoming chapters for ways to decrease your expenses.)

If your income is higher than your expenses, then put that extra money to work.

You might direct some to

- Emergency fund savings
- Debt repayment
- Sinking funds, putting money aside for known future obligations (like Christmas, vacation, or car maintenance)
- Retirement contributions

As you calculate where your dollars are going each month, the goal is to give *every* dollar a purpose.

Example: Suggested Allocation for the Remainder of Tricia's Budget:

Purpose	Amount
Emergency Fund	$250
Extra Debt Payment	$200
Short-Term Savings (car repairs, travel, etc.)	$100
Giving	$50
Fun or Treat Money	$50
Total:	$650

Do you see how this works? The goal of budgeting is that you have breathing room to prioritize things like saving, giving, and fun outings/making memories. A budget is not supposed to be something that makes you feel handcuffed.

If you are budgeting well, you are going to feel more and more like your money is going further, that it's being used much more intentionally, and that you have more ability to spend in areas that are important to you.

Step 5: Personalize Your Plan (20 Minutes)

Now, this is the hardest part for some. It's not enough to just set up a budget: You have to follow it for it to work for you! I highly recommend creating a system for tracking your spending and keeping yourself accountable.

1. **Pen and Paper**
   Simple. Effective. Just print your budget sheet that you created and track your spending by hand each week.
2. **Budgeting Apps**
   There are a number of budgeting apps (both free and paid) that sync with your bank and track spending for you. These are great if you're tech-savvy and like convenience.
3. **Spreadsheets**
   If you love numbers or want a visual, Google Sheets and Excel can be powerful tools for building custom budgets and charts.
4. **Cash Envelopes**
   These are perfect if you overspend easily. Withdraw cash for certain categories (groceries, gas, etc.) and place it in labeled envelopes. When the envelope is empty, you're done spending for the month!
5. **Hybrid System**
   Mix and match. For years, we used cash envelopes for daily spending on variable expenses and software for

tracking fixed expenses and big-picture goals. Do what works for *you.*

Setting up a budget might feel uncomfortable at first, but it gets easier with practice. And the peace that comes from knowing where your money is going? It's worth every single step.

Revisit your budget weekly at first and then every other week or monthly as following it becomes more of a habit. Adjust as needed. This is your tool and you get to make it work *for you.*

For more help setting up a budget, visit MoneySavingMom .com/budgetworksheet to download my free budgeting worksheet and get a coupon code for my course, The One-Hour Budget, which gives even more detailed help and guidance to set up a budget in just one hour!

Q & A Time

Before we close out this chapter, I want to address four of the most-asked questions I get when I talk about budgeting. If you thought of any of these as you were reading this chapter, I hope this section will help you feel more confident that budgeting can work for you!

- What if I don't make enough money to budget?
- What if my spouse doesn't want to budget?
- What if my income isn't consistent?
- What if my expenses vary every month?

Question: What If I Don't Make Enough Money to Budget?

Answer: If you've ever looked at your bank account and thought, *There's just not enough here to even bother with a budget,* I see you. I've been there.

I remember the tightest season of our marriage. It was the years when Jesse was in law school and our income barely covered the basic essentials (and not even those, some months!). Every single penny had to work hard for us, and there were many months when even buying something at the thrift store was just not in our budget.

I would watch other people purchase things freely and wonder if we'd ever get to that place. It was hard and it felt really lonely at times. And yet, I look back and see how it was in those lean years—when we were barely getting by sometimes—that we learned what a gift a budget was.

Without our budget, we would have had enormous financial strain during that season, and we would not have been able to survive without going into debt. Our budget was a compass that kept us on course. We didn't always like all the parts of the journey we were on or the sacrifices required along the way, but we knew that we wanted to get to the destination we had planned for, and a budget was what was going to get us there.

You don't wait to budget until you have "plenty of money"; you budget right where you are so you can stretch, steward, and strategize with *what you already have*.

Your desire to create a budget—even when it feels like there's not much to work with—is an act of bravery and hope. It's not the size of your budget that determines your success; it's your commitment to being intentional with whatever amount you do have.

If you're in a season when money feels impossibly tight, here's what I encourage you to do:

1. Focus on the Absolute Essentials First

When your paycheck is stretched thin, the goal is to make sure the most important needs are covered first. These are your non-negotiables, the things you must have to survive:

- **Housing** (rent or mortgage)
- **Utilities** (electricity, water, heat)
- **Food** (basic groceries, not takeout)
- **Transportation** (gas, insurance, car payment or bus fare)

Start by making sure these are covered. Everything else can be put on pause, trimmed, or creatively adjusted for now.

▸ **Tip:** Ask yourself, *Can I live without this for now if I absolutely have to?* If the answer is yes, it doesn't go in the essentials column.

2. Make a Plan for Past-Due Bills

If you're already behind, pick up the phone and start making calls. I know it feels scary, but being proactive is powerful. Ask for payment plans, hardship assistance, or grace periods. Most companies are far more willing to work with you if you reach out than if you disappear.

Be honest. Don't overpromise. But do contact them, explain your situation, and ask what they can do to work with you. You might be surprised at what they are willing to do!

3. Tap into Local Resources and Support

There is no shame in needing help. This is why food banks, church pantries, and community programs exist. Research organizations in your area that assist with groceries, rent, or utility bills. Your local government may also have programs like the federal **Low Income Home Energy Assistance Program** to help with heating and energy costs.

Asking for help or receiving help is not a sign of failure; it is utilizing all the resources at your disposal to aid you in moving toward a stronger and healthier financial situation.

4. Create a Bare-Bones Budget

Write down what's coming in and what absolutely must go out. That's your starting point. If there's still not enough to cover your basic needs, it's time to explore ways to increase income, even temporarily.

5. Look for Simple Ways to Increase Your Income

Sometimes the only way forward is to bring in more.

- Pick up a side gig like Uber or Lyft driving, food delivery, babysitting, or cleaning.
- Sell unused items in your home on Facebook Marketplace, eBay, or consignment.
- Use your skills—tutoring, writing, photography, sewing, organizing—to take on freelance or short-term work (see chapter 1 for more ideas on this).

▸ **Try this:** Post on Facebook or text a few friends saying, "I'm looking for some extra work right now to bring in additional income. I'm willing to do babysitting, cleaning, odd jobs, anything! If you hear of anything, please let me know." You never know what doors might open from one honest ask.

6. Avoid New Debt

It might feel like a credit card or payday loan is a quick fix, but it only delays your progress and deepens the financial stress. Instead, challenge yourself to get creative, be resourceful, and think outside the box! Don't sacrifice long-term stability for short-term relief.

7. Give Yourself Grace and Keep Moving Forward

Progress might feel slow. You may have to take three steps forward and two steps back. That's okay. *It's still progress.*

You are not lazy. You are not failing. You are showing up. You are doing the hard work. And it matters! A small bill paid off, an extra twenty dollars earned, a pantry meal that helped you stretch your grocery budget—these all can make more of a difference than you might realize at the time.

This hard season won't last forever. One day, you'll be the one encouraging someone else because you'll know what it's like to live on less, to make tough choices, to climb your way out. And you'll be living proof that it's possible.

Question: What If My Spouse Doesn't Want to Be on a Budget?

Answer: Even though Jesse and I were raised in financially conservative homes and had lots of pre-wedding financial talks, once we got married, it became clear: We had *very* different approaches to money.

He's the spender. I'm the saver.

He researches every purchase. I make fast decisions.

He likes high quality. I prefer the best deal.

Sound familiar?

Here's what we've learned along the way that might encourage you.

1. Accept That You're Different—and That's Okay!

You didn't marry your financial clone (thank goodness). Differences in money styles can actually be strengths *if* you stop trying to "fix" your spouse and instead look for how their perspective can complement yours.

2. Appreciate What the Other Brings to the Table

Over time, I stopped seeing Jesse's preferences as wrong and began to notice how they brought balance to my frugality. Now we're both more thoughtful with our spending. And yes, Jesse sometimes loves finding deals even more than I do!

3. Open Conversations Without Blame

Try asking questions like the following in a curious way, not a condemning or critical one:

- "What did money look like in your home growing up?"
- "What are your hopes for our financial future?"
- "What's one thing you'd change about our finances if you could?"

Then just *listen.*

4. Consider Monthly "Money Meetings"

These can be simple check-ins when you talk goals, review spending, and dream together. Keep it relaxed, kind, and pressure-free.

5. Set Shared Goals

When it's *your goal together* (not just your idea alone), your spouse is more likely to be invested. Start with smaller goals: saving for a trip, paying off one debt, or building a little emergency fund. Track your progress and celebrate wins, even tiny ones.

6. Give Grace and Breathing Room

We've found a helpful solution in our home: a monthly "blow" category. We each get a small amount to spend *guilt-free* on whatever we choose. No explanations. No judgment. This one tweak has made budgeting more sustainable for both of us.

You don't have to be perfectly in sync, but you can build *unity* over time. Listen well. Be curious. Give grace.

And remember: Budgeting isn't just about dollars and cents; it's about creating a unified partnership in your marriage.

Question: What If My Income Isn't Consistent?

Answer: This is such a great question and one I hear often. Many people assume that budgeting works only if you have a consistent paycheck that comes in like clockwork every week or two. But that simply isn't true.

Let me encourage you with this: **We've *never* had consistent income.**

When Jesse and I were first married, I worked as a waitress, and Jesse worked a part-time job. I never knew exactly how many hours I'd get or what kind of tips I'd bring home. We were trying to save every penny we could for Jesse's upcoming law school years, so we lived on as little as possible and saved the rest. A budget was key in making that work.

During law school, we juggled a few part-time jobs with unpredictable hours, and I began dabbling in online business and blogging. Some months we made a little more, other months much less. We were often barely scraping by, but we stuck with our very bare-bones budget regardless, and it helped keep us on track.

Fast forward to today: MoneySavingMom.com is our full-time family income, but even now our income still varies, often by quite a bit each month! We work with various brands and companies, and some months are full of opportunities, while others are slower. We've learned to expect that some projects won't pan out, or that what worked great one year might no longer work the next.

And once again, budgeting is what helps us weather the unpredictability.

HOW TO BUDGET WHEN YOUR INCOME ISN'T CONSISTENT

If your income is irregular like ours always has been, here's what I recommend:

1. **Build Your Budget on Your Lowest Month's Income**

   Start by identifying your *lowest-earning month* from the past year. That number becomes your baseline budget.

If your lowest month brings in $3,000, build your monthly budget around that amount.

This ensures your essential expenses (like housing, utilities, and groceries) are always covered. Everything you earn above that is *extra* and you can use it strategically (we'll talk about that in a moment).

If you don't earn anything during certain months (for instance, if you are a teacher and don't work summers), look at your annual income instead. What's your total income over the course of a year? Take that amount and shave off 20 to 30 percent to give yourself some cushion, then divide what's left by twelve. That's your monthly budgeting number.

Why 20 to 30 percent less? Because this gives you margin. Life doesn't always go according to plan, and budgeting for a little less than you *think* you'll earn reduces stress and helps you live below your means, not at the edge of them.

2. **Consult Your Budget, Not Your Bank Account**

   This mindset shift can change everything: Don't look at your bank account balance to decide if you can afford something; look at your *budget*.

   To help with this, consider depositing your income into a separate savings account. Then, each month, transfer into your checking account just what you need to cover your planned budget. This creates consistency and protects you from overspending during the higher-income months.

3. **Make Short-Term Sacrifices to Build an Emergency Fund**

   An emergency fund is especially critical when your income isn't guaranteed. Start by saving enough for one month of expenses, then work up to three to six months.

   Use any extra income in better months to build this fund. Think of your emergency savings like a bill you owe yourself and prioritize it! Yes, this might mean tightening your budget temporarily. That's okay. It's a short-term sacrifice for long-term peace of mind.

If you've already trimmed your budget as much as possible, brainstorm small ways to increase your income temporarily. Could you pick up a side job in the evenings? Offer tutoring, babysitting, or pet-sitting, or sell a few things on Facebook Marketplace? Even an extra $50 to $100 a month can add up quickly when you're focused and intentional.

4. **Create Sinking Funds for Predictable Expenses**

   Sinking funds (just a fancy term that means savings for what's to come) are your secret tool to always being prepared for expenses that don't happen monthly but can catch you off guard. These are things like car repairs, holiday gifts, or back-to-school shopping.

   A sinking fund is money you set aside gradually over time to prepare for a future, known expense. Instead of being caught off guard when that expense arrives, you're ready because you've been saving for it in small amounts ahead of time.

   Sinking funds are important because they prevent you from relying on credit cards, dipping into your emergency fund, or scrambling your monthly budget when a big expense pops up. They give you more control, lower financial anxiety, and help you stay on track with your overall financial goals. With a sinking fund, you're not just reacting to expenses, you're planning for them.

   Break these into bite-sized chunks and save toward them throughout the year. For example, if you want to spend $600 for holiday gifts, start putting $50 a month aside in January. When December hits, you'll be ready!

5. **Use the Extras Wisely**

   When you have a higher-income month, the temptation to splurge is real. But if you want long-term freedom and peace, commit to using the surplus wisely.

Here are smart ways to use it:

- Add to or replenish your emergency fund
- Pay down debt
- Save for a future goal (home down payment, retirement, travel)
- Strengthen a budget category that's tight
- Set aside for summer or holiday months when income drops

At the end of the year, review how much extra income you had and how you used it. Take time to notice your wins and use that insight to plan even better for the year ahead.

6. **Practice Gratitude and Contentment**

Budgeting is more about your mindset than it is about math. When you focus on what you *do* have and what you *can* do with it, your confidence grows and your contentment often grows right alongside it. There is always something to be grateful for, and the more you practice looking for the blessings and goodness right where you are, the more likely you will be to spot the gifts around you.

You'll be surprised at how much joy and freedom come when you trade comparison and fear for gratitude and purpose. When our perspective changes, it can completely transform how we feel about our life—even if our circumstances stay exactly the same.

You *Can* Do This!

Budgeting on an inconsistent income takes a little more intention, but it absolutely is possible. Start with your lowest-income month. Give every dollar a purpose. Build an emergency fund.

And use your extra income to give your future self peace and margin.

Even if your paycheck stops in the summer, your confidence doesn't have to. With a plan in place, you'll know exactly how to stretch and steward what you have every single month of the year.

Question: What If My Expenses Vary Every Month?

Answer: This is such a common question and one I *love* to answer because it can make such a big difference in how successful (and sustainable) your budget is.

One of the biggest hurdles I hear from women when it comes to budgeting is this:

"I just can't figure out how to plan for the stuff that doesn't happen every month!"

I get it. It's one thing to plan for your rent or car payment. But what about car repairs? Or medical co-pays? They don't follow a set schedule and the amounts can feel all over the place.

That's why we have a page dedicated to variable expenses in our budgeting worksheets (go to MoneySavingMom.com /budgetworksheets to download these), because I don't want you to forget them! When we *don't* plan ahead, these expenses often show up as financial curveballs and throw everything off.

However, with a few simple shifts, you can stay ahead of them, and even start to feel empowered and prepared when they occur.

STEP 1: IDENTIFY AND LIST YOUR VARIABLE EXPENSES

Start by looking back at the past six to twelve months of your spending. What expenses came up that weren't part of your regular monthly bills but still arose somewhat consistently?

Here are a few common categories to jog your memory:

- Gifts (birthdays, holidays, weddings)
- Car maintenance and repairs
- Medical expenses (co-pays, prescriptions)
- Annual subscriptions or membership fees
- Clothing
- Kids' activities or school supplies
- Travel or vacation spending
- Home maintenance (repairs, seasonal upkeep)

Use the Variable Expenses worksheet (at MoneySavingMom.com/budgetworksheets) to help spark ideas. Once you've listed them, group them by category to get a big-picture view of where your money tends to go "occasionally."

STEP 2: CALCULATE MONTHLY AVERAGES

Now let's make those irregular expenses more predictable. Look at what you spent in each category over the last year. Divide that total by twelve to get a monthly average. For example, if you spent $600 on car maintenance last year, aim to set aside $50 per month going forward.

If some categories spike seasonally (such as gifts in December), spread those expenses out over the whole year so they don't catch you off guard.

Budgeting ahead is one of the most powerful things you can do. Don't just hope the money will be there—**plan for it and set it aside!**

STEP 3: CREATE SINKING FUNDS

As I talked about earlier, a sinking fund is simply money you set aside each month for a future expense. Think of it as "already spoken for" money. It's not to be touched until it's needed for thc allotted purpose.

Here are a few ways you can set up your sinking funds:

Cash Envelopes

Label envelopes for each category (like gifts or clothing) and add to them each payday. This worked so well for us in the early years! We'd take the envelope to the store—and if we had only $40 in the "clothing" envelope, that's all we had to spend. (If you mostly shop online, we'll talk more about how to have a cash budget with online shopping in chapter 4.)

Separate Savings Accounts

Some banks let you create multiple savings subaccounts, which is a great digital option for tracking each fund.

Budgeting Apps

Some budgeting apps allow you to track digital sinking funds right inside your budget. After years of using cash envelopes, we now use an app to track our budget and we love it. Every dollar we earn is assigned a purpose, and when we have a larger purchase to make (like a car repair), we check our car repair sinking fund to see what's available and how much we can spend.

No matter which method you use, the point is the same: **You're setting aside money now for the expenses you know are coming later.**

That means no panic, no scrambling, and no feeling like you've failed when you need to pay for an oil change or birthday gift because you already planned for it.

STEP 4: BUILD FLEXIBILITY INTO YOUR BUDGET

Variable expenses are just that, *variable*! Even with the best planning, there will be months when something unexpected pops up or a category costs more than you thought it would.

Don't panic! Flexibility is the secret sauce that helps you stick with your budget long-term.

Here are a few ways to add that wiggle room:

Add a Miscellaneous Category

This can be a small buffer each month for the odds and ends that don't fit neatly into other categories. Jesse and I also each have personal "blow money," as we call it. This is an amount we can spend however we want, no questions asked. Sometimes we use it for fun, sometimes for surprises like a last-minute gift.

Roll Over Unused Funds

If you don't use all of a sinking fund in a given month, let it roll over. This builds up a cushion for when that category *does* need more. For example, we might go months without using our car repair sinking fund and then one repair wipes out half of it. But because we were consistent in adding to it, we don't have to worry when our car breaks down suddenly or needs a pretty significant repair.

Reassess Regularly

Life changes, and so will your budget. Review things monthly and make small adjustments. If you keep needing to shift money between categories (we call it "robbing Peter to pay Paul"), it might be time to adjust how much you're setting aside in each one.

Remember, Give Yourself Grace

Again, budgeting isn't about perfection; it's about progress.

There will be months when you forget something. You'll overspend in a category. Something unexpected will derail your best-laid plans. When that happens, don't give up.

Instead, ask yourself

- *What can I learn from this?*
- *What can I do right now to course correct?*

Budgeting is a skill, and every "mistake" is an opportunity to get stronger and wiser with your money.

Variable expenses aren't the enemy of your budget, they're just the reason your budget needs to work *with* real life, not against it.

By identifying your irregular expenses, calculating an average, creating sinking funds, and giving yourself some flexibility, you'll not only stay on track, you'll likely start to feel more confident and in control than ever before.

And the next time a birthday party pops up last-minute and you need to buy a gift, or your car makes a funny noise and you know you need to have a mechanic check it, you can smile and say, "Good thing I planned for this."

Your Budget = Your Priorities in Action

Now that you've created your budget, let's bring it full circle: back to your financial priorities. Remember Habit #2? You took the time to get clear on what matters most to you—the things you want your money to *do* for you. Your budget is the tool that makes those dreams practical. Every line item is a decision. And each decision is a step toward the life you're working to build.

A healthy budget isn't just a list of numbers; it's a reflection of your *values*. That's why I always encourage people to ask: "**Does my spending reflect what matters most to me?**"

If you say family time is a priority, are you budgeting for that weekly coffee date with your teen? If giving is important, does your budget include space to be generous? You want your budget to align with your priorities and remind you to make consistent, thoughtful choices that match your heart.

Your Budget in Action = Your Priorities in Motion

At the end of the day, budgeting isn't really about money. It's about your *mission*. It's about using what you have—no matter how little or how much—with purpose. That's what Habit #2 taught us: When you know your priorities, you can build a life that reflects them.

This chapter is where those priorities meet action. Maybe for you, that means building up your emergency fund. Maybe it's cutting back on eating out so you can give more generously or finally take that family trip.

For us, I remember one month early in our marriage when we had seven dollars in fun money left for the month . . . and we used most of it to rent two $0.50 movies at Family Video and buy a $2.99 entree meal and a $0.99 kids' entree meal at Long John Silver's with coupons. It wasn't much, but it reminded us that we were on the same page and that joy didn't have to be expensive.

You're not budgeting to limit your life. You're budgeting to **live your life**—on purpose, with calmness, and with progress you can see and feel.

In the next three chapters, I am going to give you my very best strategies to help you follow through with the budget you have created. I'll help you to maximize the mileage of your money, get the biggest bang for your buck, and learn how to set up irresistible accountability so that the budget you create isn't just a good idea on paper . . . it actually transforms the rest of your life!

Journaling Prompt

Take a few quiet moments and jot down **three things you want your money to do for you this month.** Is it saving money for an upcoming family vacation? Covering a needed repair? Making a donation to a cause you are passionate about? Write it down. Let this serve as your guide as you plan your budget for this month. Make sure the numbers on paper reflect the priorities that are important to you.

Habit #4

Use Cash for Everything

Spend Only the Money You Already Have

My hair was perfectly sprayed. My makeup professionally done. I sat in a cold, dimly lit concrete room, waiting for the producer to call me onto the set. My heart pounded in my chest, and I could feel the nervous energy pulsing through every inch of my body.

Just one week earlier, I'd received a surprising email. The producers of a well-known national financial TV show had invited me to fly to New York City to be on a segment. It was my first time appearing on a show of that size, hosted by someone who was so widely respected, and truthfully, I felt completely out of my league.

As I waited to be fitted with a mic pack, I watched the guests ahead of me on the monitor. They rattled off statistics, discussed complex economic trends, and used terms I didn't even recognize. All I could think was, *What is a homeschooled girl from Kansas—who never even went to college—doing on a show like this?*

I wanted to run. I seriously considered slipping out the side door before they called my name. But I stayed. I walked out, went live in front of millions of people . . . and shared confidently (even if I was faking most of that confidence!) why I don't use a credit card—and why I've never had one.

The host was kind and encouraging overall, though he definitely played devil's advocate, questioning why I would choose such a countercultural lifestyle in a credit-driven world. Ultimately, I think he was just really fascinated that someone who lives a very normal life with all the modern conveniences of running water, cars, electricity, cell phones, and internet would choose to live life without a credit card.

In this chapter, I'm going to share more of what I talked about on that show—and yes, I'm going to do my best to convince you that you, too, should only spend money you already have for everyday purchases. But before you skip this chapter or shut this book altogether, know this: I'm not here to tell you credit cards are evil. I'm not even going to suggest you need to cut yours up.

My hope in talking about using cash and why I don't have a credit card is just to encourage you to pause and think more intentionally before you swipe . . . and maybe—just maybe—inspire you to try using only cash or a debit card for a little while.

No Card—and No Credit

People are often shocked when they learn I've never had a credit card. It's not something I go around announcing, but it comes up from time to time in conversations.

Their eyes usually widen. "Wait, you've *never* had a credit card? Like, ever?"

"Nope," I'll respond with a smile.

"Not even when you were younger—like ten or twenty years ago or something?"

"No, really and truly. I've never had a credit card."

At that point, people typically look at me like I've just said I've never used running water or don't know what the internet is. Here's the thing: Living without a credit card in today's world can feel archaic, old-fashioned, and maybe just a bit ludicrous. But I've made peace with being a little unorthodox.

The upside? I've never had credit card debt. No minimum payments hanging over my head. No interest piling up. No anxiety every time I open a statement. That kind of freedom—both financial and mental—is something I deeply value and don't take for granted.

The downside? I have zero credit. Literally. My credit score is nonexistent. Since we've always paid cash for everything, it hasn't caused many issues, but it has created a few hurdles.

For example, when I went to get an iPhone the first time, they wanted a $500 deposit. We ended up putting it in Jesse's name because he has a secured credit card and has built up some credit.

In addition, some rental car companies won't rent to you without a credit card. And forget about renting in one location and returning it to another with just a debit card. (That's something we learned the hard way!) When we were first married, we even had to have one of our dads cosign on our apartment lease because we had absolutely no credit history.

For me, though, living without a credit card has worked just fine, and I'd rather keep it that way.

That said, I don't believe credit cards are inherently bad. I know plenty of people who use them wisely. They pay them off in full each month and reap rewards like airline miles and hotel points. If that's you, and it's not causing stress or overspending, I'm not here to talk you out of it.

In fact, we've encouraged our older kids to start with a secured credit card when they become adults. We recommend that they use it for boring purchases like gas so there is no temptation to overspend while they work to build a credit history.

I don't love that credit plays such a big role in our culture, but the reality is that it does. So I believe it's wise to be proactive.

That said, if you're feeling stretched thin, if you are using your credit card as a crutch, or if balances are weighing you down, I want to invite you to try a new approach, even if for just a little while.

In this chapter, I'm challenging you to adopt one simple but powerful mindset shift:

Only spend money you already have and have already budgeted for.

That's what **Habit #4: Use Cash for Everything** is all about.

What Is a Secured Credit Card?

A secured credit card is one that requires a refundable cash deposit—often starting at $200 or $300—as collateral. Your deposit usually becomes your credit limit. Unlike a debit card, secured credit cards report your activity to the credit bureaus, helping build or improve your credit history.

But why would someone who has avoided debt and been financially wise choose to open one? Because having no credit history can make it difficult to rent an apartment, qualify for good insurance rates, or get approved for a mortgage. A secured credit card lets you build a healthy credit profile with minimal risk, especially if you pay off the balance in full each month and never carry debt. It's a smart, controlled way to show lenders you're responsible, even if you've never borrowed a dime before.

If you are going to get a credit card, I highly recommend obtaining a secured credit card and using it for expenses that are essential, such as gas and utilities. This way, you can build credit while not being tempted to overspend.

What Do I Mean By "Cash"? Do Only Green Bills Count or Does That Include Debit Cards?

Let me be clear: Using cash for everything doesn't mean you need to carry around stacks of twenties and fifties for every purchase (though I *do* think there's value in using physical cash in some situations—but we'll get to that in a bit). What it *does* mean is that you spend only money you already have, either in your wallet or in your bank account.

In the previous chapter, we walked through how to set up a budget. This chapter builds on that foundation. Because if you truly want to stick to your budget, you need to commit to only spending what you have.

That's the beauty of using cash! It's like a built-in accountability system. Why? Because it's virtually impossible to overspend when you're only using real money. Yes, it's true you can take physical cash you've budgeted for one category and use it elsewhere, which can throw off your plan, but even then, you're not spending more than you have. You're simply reallocating what's already in your hands. And that small difference makes a big impact.

The Heart Behind This Habit

Let's be honest: This habit might feel extreme at first. You might be thinking, *Use cash for everything? Really?* In a world where swiping, tapping, and one-click checkouts are the norm, using actual cash or even choosing to only spend from your checking account can seem antiquated.

But before you write it off, I want to gently invite you to lean in. Because this habit is not about punishing yourself for past money mistakes or living in scarcity.

It's about *freedom.*

It's about stepping into *clarity* and *control*. It's about anchoring your spending in reality instead of hopeful guesses, wishful thinking, or future paychecks. It's about giving yourself the confidence of knowing exactly where you stand financially, so you can make decisions with confidence instead of anxiety or guilt.

There's a big difference between spending real money and spending *future* money. Future money is the credit card swipe you promise to pay off next month. It's the "buy now, pay later" button that seems harmless in the moment. It's overdrafting your account because you assume your paycheck will hit in time. These decisions may feel convenient now, but they often lead to stress, uncertainty, and regret later.

On the other hand, when you spend only what you *actually* have, something powerful happens: you *feel free*. Truly free. Free from the pressure of juggling due dates and balances. Free from wondering if you're falling behind. Free to breathe easier because your bills are covered, your savings are growing, and you're not living on borrowed time or borrowed money.

That's why I love this habit. It's not about deprivation. It's about peace. And you might be surprised at how empowering it feels to spend only what you have—no guilt, no guessing, no going backward.

Just real progress, one dollar at a time.

As we continue this chapter, know that I'm not here to convince you to carry cash for every transaction (though I'll share some great reasons that can be helpful). I simply want to invite you to consider the heart behind this habit and hopefully help you discover that this might be a path worth exploring.

The Debt-Free Legacy That Shaped Me

I shared in chapter 2 how my grandpa taught my dad to never go into debt for anything except a mortgage, and that my dad took that advice to heart and went a step further. As I recounted, when I was a little girl, my parents not only paid off their mortgage but also scrimped and saved every penny so they could buy land and build a house debt-free.

Seeing the sacrifices my parents made, and the freedom that came from not owing anything to anyone, deeply shaped how I thought about money. I witnessed with my own eyes how living within your means provides you the margin to be a generous giver. That's the mindset Jesse and I took into our marriage and that led us to the decision that he would go to law school *without* taking on any debt.

Let me tell you, it sounded a whole lot more inspiring than it actually felt while living it out. It meant we had only one car, lived in a basement apartment with a tiny galley kitchen, and we could plug the vacuum into one outlet and pretty much vacuum the entire apartment without needing to move the plug—because our apartment was that small!

It meant we worked a bunch of different side hustles and worked more than full-time hours pretty much six days every week. It meant we chose to make do with what we had and rarely buy anything that wasn't a necessity. It meant spending only $25 to $30 a week on groceries for all our meals (and getting really creative to make that work).

It meant finding free things to do for fun instead of spending money on activities. It meant using the library for much of our entertainment. It meant rarely ever going out to eat. It meant using cloth diapers and having only six outfits per size for our first baby for the first year.

But we did it. And that decision planted the seed for an even bigger one later: We set a goal to pay cash for our first house.

Now, deciding you are going to try to stay out of debt in college and law school is one thing. People think you are strange, for sure, but saying you are going to save up to pay 100 percent down for your first house puts you on a whole new level of weird to most people.

In fact, it felt like many of our acquaintances kind of thought we'd lost our minds.

"There is no way you can do that in this economy."

"It's ridiculous to throw money down the drain by paying for rent every month! Just get a mortgage! It's so much smarter!"

We heard these comments from well-meaning folks again and again. And I know our plan did seem pretty farfetched in today's world.

But, since we had learned to live really simply in law school, because we didn't have debt, because our income had started steadily increasing during and after law school, we chose to continue to live on very little so we could save aggressively. We also chose to buy in an area where housing was less expensive (Kansas), and we looked for a starter home. Our goal was to buy a very small and inexpensive home, pay cash for it, and then save up more money, sell that home, and use the money from the sale plus our savings to buy a home a bit larger. We planned to do this a few times as our family grew.

We ended up reaching our house savings goal in less than three years, which was a huge surprise to us because it was quite a bit sooner than we expected and planned it would be! I truly believe we never would have worked so hard or thought so creatively if we hadn't been so motivated by that original goal.

No, I Don't Think Credit Cards Are Evil

Years later, we have zero regrets about our decision to save up and pay cash for our first house. Yes, it meant many sacrifices and a lot of thinking outside the box. Yes, it meant renting when all our friends were buying houses. But it also has meant that we are now reaping the fruit of those years of hard work and scrimping and saving.

We've continued to choose to not have a mortgage and to live on significantly less than we make so we can save aggressively and live generously. We still track every dollar we spend and have a clear written budget for every month. I still don't like math or spreadsheets. (I don't think that's going to change!) I still don't have a credit card. And at this point, I don't have plans to ever get one.

We look back and see how much margin and flexibility we've experienced because of our commitment to live debt-free. It has allowed us to make business pivots, move across the country, and say yes to opportunities we might otherwise have had to pass up.

It has also helped us stay laser-focused on what matters to us—our priorities, our people, and our purpose. We've been able to live simply, have breathing room in our budget, and walk in peace rather than pressure.

I know our way isn't the only way.

But if you're constantly feeling behind, discouraged, or overwhelmed by your finances, I want to quietly challenge you: Maybe it's time to do something different.

Why This Habit Matters More Than You Think

It's easy to swipe a card and not think much about it, especially when it's "just" $30 here or $75 there. But those small swipes can quietly snowball into a burden that weighs more heavily than we ever intended.

Let's put it into perspective.

In the US, the average amount of credit card debt per American, as of September 2025, is $6,523.[1] So married couples are carrying an average of $13,000 in credit card debt.

That number alone is sobering, but the true cost is in what happens over time. If you make only the minimum payment on that $13,000 balance—let's say $300 a month—with a

22 percent interest rate, it will take you seven years and four months to pay it off. And by the time it's paid off, you'll have shelled out an additional $13,124.50 in interest.

Let that sink in: You borrowed $13,000 and paid back $26,124.50— over 200 percent of the original amount.

That's $13,000-plus that could have gone toward something so much more meaningful: savings, experiences with your family, paying off your car, giving generously, or even just breathing room in your budget.

And this is just credit card debt. So many people also owe money on their vehicles, have a mortgage, have medical debt, and other loans. It can add up to such a heavy load just paying interest every month on all your payments!

It's easy to fall into the trap of "I'll just put it on the card or get a loan or do the payment plan for now and figure it out later," especially if that is what has been modeled for you and what you are seeing almost everyone around you do. But this is why **Habit #4: Use Cash for Everything** matters so much.

When you commit to only spending what's *already* in your account (not what you *hope* will be there later!), you start living from a place of strength instead of stress.

You stop paying for your past and start building toward your future.

You get your margin back.

You gain peace of mind.

And slowly but surely, you start to feel free.

It's Okay to Be Different

Maybe the traditional path isn't working for you. Maybe it's time to try something unconventional. Maybe you need a reset.

You don't have to live like everyone else. You don't have to take on debt just because "everyone" does. You don't have to stay stuck in patterns that leave you exhausted.

You get to choose a new way forward.

It might mean stepping out of your comfort zone. It might mean making some short-term sacrifices. It might mean people don't understand your choices.

But it might also mean joy, freedom, and the ability to say yes to the things that matter most to you.

Take the Thirty-Day Cash-Only Challenge

Want to try it out? In just thirty days, you might change your life, or at least uncover some unexpected aha moments for you around money.

Here's how to do the Thirty-Day Cash-Only Challenge:

1. **Decide which parts of your budget will be cash only.** I recommend your grocery budget for sure, but also maybe you want to commit to cash-only for a few other areas where you often are tempted to overspend, maybe eating out or clothing/shoe purchases. You get to decide and there are no right or wrong answers to which budget categories you choose.
2. **Go back to the budget you set up in the previous chapter** (and are hopefully using on a daily basis now) and figure out what amount(s) you have budgeted for those categories for the next thirty days; keep it simple and just go with whatever you would budget for a month or four weeks.
3. **Head to the bank and withdraw the amount of money you've budgeted,** then figure out a system for organizing it (cash envelopes? In your safe?) I recommend not bringing your entire monthly allotment when you go to the store, but just what you've budgeted for that week or what you think you'll use for that shopping trip.

4. **Leave your credit cards and debit cards at home.** If you think you'd be tempted to use it (or you usually pay with it), consider disabling Apple Pay or Tap to Pay on your phone. Only take your envelope of cash with you to the store.
5. **Add things up as you go.** Use your calculator on your phone (or you can bring an old-school calculator) to track your total while you shop. Keep a running total on it (you could also write it down on your grocery list or notes app on your phone in case you lose the total on the calculator—as I have done before). You'll likely start noticing how much things really cost and begin second-guessing impulse buys, hunting for better deals, and getting creative if your list is longer than your budget.
6. **Pay with cash at checkout.** See if your spending drops any. If anything, I bet that your awareness will go up! (Note: You can also get a prepaid card to use if you ever run into a situation where a retailer won't take cash.)
7. **Learn and adjust.** Will this challenge magically fix everything? Probably not. But I can pretty much guarantee you'll learn something valuable, and you just might be amazed at how much you save.

The Psychology of Cash Spending

Let's talk about why using cash can make a difference, not just practically, but psychologically. This isn't merely a personal preference or an old-fashioned budgeting style. There's solid research, neuroscience, and lived experience to back it up. And once you understand the *why*, I think you might be more motivated to give it a try.

When you spend paper cash, it feels different. Behavioral economists call this the "pain of paying."[2] Studies show that handing over physical bills activates the areas of the brain associated with physical pain, creating a small but measurable sense of loss. That's not just a figure of speech; it's visible in brain scans.[3]

One well-known MIT study found that people were willing to pay up to 64 percent more for the same item when using a credit card instead of cash.[4] Why? Could it be because swiping a card feels less real, less personal, and (most importantly) less painful? More recent research from MIT Sloan using fMRI scans found that credit card purchases activate the brain's reward centers (the striatum), which can potentially "step on the gas" and encourage spending, while cash doesn't trigger the same response.[5]

Other studies back up these findings. In consumer surveys, people report being twice as likely to make impulse purchases with a card versus cash.[6]

When you use cash, you feel the loss in a tangible way, which can actually be a positive. It serves as a sort of built-in speed bump, motivating you to pause, assess, and ask, "Is this really worth it?" That extra moment of awareness can be enough to stop an impulse purchase or redirect the money toward a goal that matters more to you.

I remember when we were first married and our grocery budget was super tight. We had budgeted thirty dollars to pay for all our groceries for the week. Some weeks, we didn't even have that amount because our income was so sparse during that season. Because I used cash to buy our groceries, I was never tempted to overspend. Instead, it challenged me to get creative. I loved seeing how well we could eat for how little.

As I put an item in my cart, I would add it to the running total on my calculator (that was before we had calculators on our phones). Sometimes, there wasn't enough to pay for everything I wanted to buy. Because I knew that I had only the cash in

Why I Love Using Cash

1. **Cash helps you stick to your budget.**
Yes, it's possible to blow through cash. But when the cash is gone, it's gone. There's a built-in boundary that forces you to pace yourself. If you spend your grocery money too quickly, you have to make do until your next budget cycle. It's a natural accountability system.
2. **Cash makes you stop and think.**
Handing over physical bills makes you pause. There's a level of accountability that's hard to achieve when you're just swiping. The transaction feels more real, and that thoughtfulness can lead to wiser decisions.
3. **Cash keeps you focused in the present.**
Many people say they treat their credit cards like cash—and maybe you do. But unless you're setting aside the full amount of each purchase in a separate account immediately, you're not truly treating it like cash. You're spending based on the assumption that future you will have the money. But what if your income changes? What if there's an unexpected emergency?
Cash forces you to spend based on what you *actually have right now*, not what you hope you'll have later.
4. **Cash means you never owe anyone.**
When you pay with cash, you don't have to worry about interest, due dates, or minimum payments. You buy it, it's yours, and you move on. There's freedom in that. And sometimes, the wait to save up for something can make the purchase that much sweeter.

hand to spend, I would evaluate every purchase carefully before adding it to my cart to make sure it was truly worth the cost.

While spending only what you already have keeps you aware of what is realistic and doable within your budget, it also eliminates the temptation to borrow from the future or justify purchases with a vague promise to "figure it out later." There's no fuzzy math when you're dealing with real dollars. You see what you have, you know what you can spend, and you adjust accordingly. That clarity builds confidence.

If you've ever felt that money slips through your fingers or you end the month wondering where it went, this habit can be a simple but powerful reset. It's not about punishment; it's about *permission*:

Permission to stop the cycle of unconscious spending.

Permission to slow down.

Permission to spend in a way that truly aligns with your values and priorities.

You don't need a degree in behavioral science to make this work. You just need a willingness to try it. Pick one category (like groceries or dining out) to use cash for this month. Pay attention to how it feels. You might be surprised by how quickly you see a shift in your awareness—and your spending.

Troubleshooting: Common Questions and Pushbacks

Because groceries and living costs are higher than ever, using cash is more powerful than ever. It challenges you to know your priorities and forces creativity, even in tough times. That said, any time I promote using cash, I am always met with resistance. So let's talk through the real-life hesitations that might come up; I hope to offer grace-filled solutions to help you move forward with confidence.

"I pay for everything online. What should I do?"

This is one of the most common concerns I hear. I get it! In today's world, so much of our spending happens digitally. If that's your situation, consider using a *digital cash* system. For example, you can preload grocery funds onto a store-specific gift card (like one for Walmart or Target) or use a prepaid debit card that's loaded only with your budgeted amount. This creates the same spending boundaries that physical cash provides but in a format that works with online shopping.

"What about emergencies?"

This is an important question. First, I want to reiterate that using cash isn't about pretending emergencies don't happen. It's about helping you to be more thoughtful with your money so that you have a lot fewer emergencies.

As soon as you possibly can, begin setting aside money for a one-month emergency fund. If you need to work a side job or sell items you own in order to come up with that amount, do it. It will be worth it for your peace of mind.

I'd challenge you to not stop at saving up for only one month of emergency expenses. Cut back to bare-bones basics and work extra hours for a season to save up at least three months' worth of expenses. That way, if a pay cut or job loss happens, or a big unexpected expense arises, you have a cushion to carry you instead of your winding up in complete panic and desperation mode.

"Isn't cash unsafe or inconvenient?"

Carrying around envelopes of money may sound a little risky. But remember, cash is just a tool. And like any tool, how you use it matters. You don't need to carry hundreds of dollars with you at all times. Bring only what you need. Keep it tucked away securely in your wallet or a zippered pouch.

You might be surprised how quickly you get used to it and how much more purposeful your spending becomes. Yes, if someone steals it, you likely can't get it back, but I would guess you'll end up saving hundreds of dollars a year by using cash, and the savings will outweigh the risks involved—especially if you only bring a small amount of cash with you at a time!

"Can't I just be disciplined with my card?"

Yes, you *can*—and some people truly are! But if you've struggled to stay on track in the past, there's a good chance that removing the swipe-and-go ease of card spending could be the reset your brain needs. Handing over cash creates a little bit of friction that can help you slow down, evaluate your choices, and build stronger spending habits.

For a number of years, our family used a hybrid system for our expenditures. We had cash envelopes for items we would typically buy locally and used debit cards or online bill pay for our utility bills, insurance, and other bills paid on a monthly basis. This worked well for us for many years, and it helped us to be very disciplined with our spending and to stick with our budget.

A question people often ask when I talk about cash envelopes is, "If you use cash only for clothing, food and so forth, does this mean you can't purchase any items from your cash envelope categories online?" Well, no.

We used gift cards to pay for some of our online purchases or we would buy online with our debit card and then refund the money from our cash envelope to our bank account.

It might seem like a hassle to refund the money to your bank account, but if you need that extra step to be mindful about your purchases and stick with your budget, this is definitely something to consider. Instead of just jumping on a good deal because you're afraid it might not be available for long, it forces you to think through whether it's a good deal *for you*, meaning it's something you need or have been planning to purchase, something you can afford in that budget category, and something you will use. And because it's a little more time-consuming, you may find you end up talking yourself out of the purchase!

What About Trying a Virtual Envelope System?

If messing with cash seems tedious to you, a great alternative is to use a Virtual Cash Envelope system through a program like YNAB.com (You Need a Budget) or EveryDollar.com.

These apps allow you to set up your cash envelopes or budget categories and then deduct your purchases throughout the month. This way, you can always have a running total of how much you've spent and how much you have left in each budget category.

The benefits of using this system are that you can keep better tabs on what you're spending your money on and when you're spending it, and how you're doing on your budget overall at a glance. It's also nice because you don't have to share cash envelopes if you're like our family and both spouses pitch in with grocery and other shopping throughout the month.

The drawbacks are that you are swiping a debit card, which means you can more easily go over budget than when you are using cash. Plus, it requires one more step than cash because you have to input the data after each shopping trip and track how much you have left in each budget category.

Living with Margin and Mindfulness

When we choose to use only the money we actually have (whether that's physical cash or a carefully managed debit account), we're doing more than just making a financial decision.

We're choosing to live with *margin* and *mindfulness*.

Margin is what gives you breathing room. It's what helps you sleep better at night, knowing there's money in the account—and not a pit in your stomach from wondering whether a surprise expense will send you spiraling. Living with margin doesn't mean you never spend; it means you spend *on purpose*, in a way that aligns with what matters most.

That's why this habit ties back so powerfully to your values that we talked about in the previous chapter. Using cash (or treating your debit card like cash) helps you say yes only to what truly matters. It makes you pause, reflect, and consider, *Is this how I want to spend my limited resources?* That pause alone is powerful. It's not about guilt; it's about prioritizing what matters most to you and your family.

This habit also supports the other habits we've already talked about. It helps you *stick to your budget* because you can only spend what's in the envelope or the account. It helps with *managing irregular income* because it forces you to work with what you have in front of you. And it supports *values-based spending* because it slows you down long enough to consider each choice through the lens of your priorities.

Cash = Clarity

Here's the big takeaway: You don't have to be ruled by swipes, overdrafts, or hopeful spending. You can live differently. Using only cash or a debit card brings *clarity*, *calm*, and even *joy*. It reminds you that you're in control of your money, not the other way around.

You're not using cash to limit your life; you're using it to build the life you want. One purposeful purchase at a time. One margin-filled week at a time. One thoughtful decision at a time. And the best part? You already have everything you need to begin, right in your own hands.

If you're someone who has wanted to be financially healthy in the past but didn't quite have footing to pull it off, the next habit is going to help you gain the traction to succeed this time!

Journaling Prompt

When you think of trying a Thirty-Day Cash-Only Challenge, do you feel any resistance to the idea? If so, what specifically do you feel? Where do you think this resistance is coming from? What do you think you might learn from trying this challenge?

Habit #5

Create Irresistible Accountability

Identify Your Style and Tailor a Plan That Works for You

Eight months ago, I did something that scared me. I faced a lifelong fear and walked into my very first gym class.

Now, this might not seem like a big deal to some, but for me? It was huge.

You see, I've always believed I wasn't "a gym person." I was the girl who got a C in physical education at my little Christian school in second grade. The one who dreaded running laps. The one who felt uncoordinated and out of place anytime physical activity was involved.

That belief followed me well into adulthood. Like a quiet narrative, it had whispered things like, *You don't belong in a gym. You're not coordinated like gym people are. It'll be too hard and you'll make a fool of yourself.*

So for more than twenty-five years, I let fear sit in the driver's seat. I told myself I'd stick out. That I wouldn't be able to keep up. That everyone else would somehow know exactly what to do while I floundered.

But then someone messaged me something that stuck: **"The hardest part is walking through the door."**

And isn't that true in so many areas of life? Fear tries to convince us we can't. That we'll fail. That we're not enough.

But bravery says, "Just try." So I did. I showed up. Heart pounding, hands a little shaky, grabbing the lightest weights I could find. And I reminded myself, *You're allowed to be a beginner.*

And guess what? I loved it. I (mostly) kept up. Yes, I messed up some moves, but I had fun, I got in a great workout, and I pushed myself. The instructor was encouraging and kind. And I walked out of that room not just proud of my effort but also deeply moved because I had finally stopped letting fear call the shots.

I went back three more times that week. And I've kept going multiple times every week since. I've even gotten some of my friends to come with me!

So why am I telling you this story when the habit we're digging into in this chapter is *accountability*?

Because accountability often starts the same way—with one brave, shaky step to show up. Most of the growth in our lives? It doesn't come from getting everything right. It comes from consistently choosing *not to go it alone.*

When I work out at home, I tend to quit after fifteen or twenty minutes (or sometimes even less). I tell myself, *You worked up a good sweat. That's enough.* Or, *You're tired and have a dozen other things to do. You can call it good.*

But in a class, surrounded by other people pushing through alongside me and with an encouraging instructor cheering us on, I keep going. I don't quit when it gets hard. I don't give up when I'm tired. I push through. And I'm seeing the results to prove it. (I still can't believe the muscle definition I've gained in just a few short months.)

That's what irresistible accountability looks like. And no, in case you were worried, you don't have to sign up at a gym to experience it!

In this chapter, we're going to explore how to recreate that same kind of consistency and follow-through in your finances—the kind that doesn't come from willpower alone, but from support, encouragement, and showing up with others.

Why Accountability Works (and Why You Might Be Avoiding It)

Let's be honest: The word *accountability* can carry some baggage. Maybe it brings to mind performance reviews, awkward check-ins, or someone wagging their finger at you when you fall short.

But real accountability, the kind that helps you grow, isn't about shame or pressure.

It's about encouragement. It's about honesty. It's about connection. It's about the motivation to keep going, to follow through and experience the amazing results of actually doing that thing you've wanted to do for a really long time.

When it's done right, accountability becomes an invitation, not a burden. It's someone standing beside you, gently nudging you forward when you're tempted to shrink back. It's having a trusted voice that reminds you why you started and believes you can keep going, even when you're unsure.

Human behavior is shaped by community. Study after study shows we're more likely to stick with our goals when someone else knows about them.[1]

For example, a field experiment published in *Management Science* found that participants who received a gym attendance incentive only when they went with a friend increased their visits by 35 percent and were twice as likely to show up than those who received the incentive going solo.[2] Having someone checking in with you makes it easier to keep going because you enjoy the social side and don't want to let your friend down.

We also know that simply telling someone your goal boosts your odds of success. The *Journal of Applied Psychology* found that people have greater commitment to their goals and perform better overall when they state their goals out loud to someone whose opinion they esteem and respect.[3]

There's a reason people train better with a workout buddy, eat healthier when someone's checking in, or save more money when they know they'll be asked how it's going. We are wired for connection and that includes financial growth.

Our brains respond to social accountability because we get a genuine reward when we keep a promise to someone else, and we feel uneasy at the thought of letting them down. Research shows that meeting commitments triggers the same reward centers in our brain that light up for other positive experiences.[4]

At the same time, we're wired to avoid losses. This includes the loss of social approval, so letting someone down feels especially uncomfortable. Knowing this makes it clear why sharing a goal with a friend or group can make us more likely to follow through.

But I realize you might still feel hesitant. Maybe you're thinking,

I don't want to be a burden.

I don't want anyone to see how messy this part of my life is.

I've tried this before . . . and failed.

Your feelings are real and they're valid. Remember, in chapter 3 we explored how our present-day fears around money often can be related to things in our past—things we many times don't even realize

That's what it was like for me with the gym.

For years, I didn't make the connection that I had let a C+ on a second-grade PE report card whisper all sorts of lies into my heart. Lies about who I was, what I was capable of, and where I belonged. I didn't know that two awkward years in elementary school gym class—my only experience in a formal school setting since I was homeschooled for the rest of my education—had planted a quiet, persistent belief that I was uncoordinated, incapable, and not someone who had the physical ability to participate in a class at a gym.

But once I started digging a little deeper into why I was so afraid to walk into a gym, I began to connect the dots. That fear wasn't just about weights or workouts; it was about identity. It was about how I saw myself.

And when I finally saw the truth? Something lit up inside of me.

No more, I told myself. *I will not let one tiny letter on a decades-old report card dictate what I believe about myself. I'm walking in that door, and I'm going to do my best.*

However, while this resolve and internal pep talk was helpful, I knew that if I was going to follow through with it, I'd need some accountability—because recognizing the root of my fear didn't remove the sheer panic I felt at the thought of working out in a group of people, even if they were strangers. I still had these deep-seated beliefs that I would stick out, that it would be obvious I was the only one who didn't belong, and that everyone else would know how to do the workouts while I was an uncoordinated mess.

So here's what I did to provide irresistible accountability to walk through that gym door and go to the class:

I enlisted my teen daughter to go with me as my "emotional support person."

I signed up for the class on the gym's app.

I shared my fear on Instagram the morning I was planning to go to the class and told my audience I was committed to going that night.

I posted again right before I headed into the class that I was doing it.

I picked a spot at the back—so it was less awkward.

I told the instructor that I was brand-new.

I decided ahead of time that the only goal for the class time was to do my best and to stay for the entire class. This was not about trying to push myself to the max physically. It was enough of an emotional and mental stretch just for me to be there and not walk out halfway through.

And I did! And I've kept going back consistently, even if I don't have my daughter or a friend going with me. (And—to my great surprise—I sometimes even pick a spot near the front of the class now.) That's the heart of irresistible accountability. You start out by making it as easy as possible to show up and do the thing and follow through with your goal.

When you walk through the door where there will be a group of people doing the thing you're scared to do, when you tell a friend you are doing something, or post about your goal online, you have given yourself a huge boost in the right direction. And momentum breeds momentum. So do yourself a favor by setting yourself up for the greatest success possible by putting accountability in place.

When you find the right kind of support, the kind that cheers you on while you're still figuring it out, that's where real transformation happens.

Let's talk about how to find *your* kind of accountability.

Choose Your Accountability Style

Here's the good news: There's no one-size-fits-all answer when it comes to accountability. Some people thrive with regular check-ins with a friend. Others do best when they're part of a motivated group. And some people, especially introverts or independent thinkers, find creative ways to hold *themselves* accountable and that works beautifully.

The point isn't *how* you stay accountable. It's *that* you stay accountable.

Let's explore three simple styles you can choose from—and you don't have to pick just one!

Option 1: One-on-One Support

This could be your spouse, a trusted friend, a mentor, or even a coach. The key? Choose someone who is

- Safe (they don't shame or judge)
- Supportive (they believe in your growth)
- Consistent (they'll actually follow up)

This kind of support works best when you're honest about your goals and open to checking in regularly. It's not about dumping guilt or pressure; it's about inviting someone to walk beside you.

Try this: "Hey, I'm working on sticking to a weekly grocery budget. Would you be willing to check in with me each Friday just to ask how it's going?"

Option 2: Group Accountability

There's power in momentum and mutual encouragement. Whether it's a money challenge, a small group, a text thread, or an online community, being part of something bigger helps you keep going, especially on the days when motivation runs low.

You get fresh ideas, honest encouragement, and that "me too" feeling that reminds you you're not alone.

Try this: Join or start a thirty-day savings challenge with friends. Create a group chat where you share daily wins, struggles, and tips.

Option 3: Self-Accountability Tools

If you're someone who thrives on independence or prefers quiet reflection, self-accountability *can* work, as long as you set up a rhythm that keeps you focused and consistent.

Try weekly check-ins with yourself using journal prompts, a spreadsheet, a habit tracker (go to MoneySavingMom.com/habits to download a free version and my free class on habit tracking), an app you can use to track, or a simple notebook. Use visual trackers to see your progress and mark the milestones. And be honest with yourself about what's working and what's not.

Try this: Set a reminder every Sunday to review your money wins, challenges, and goals. Use a simple template like

- What worked?
- What didn't?
- What will I try to do differently this week?

No matter which style fits you best, here's the most important part: **Don't go it alone.**

Yes, self-accountability can be powerful, but support adds staying power. Whether it's a friend you check in with monthly, an online group, or a mentor you admire from afar, find a way to stay connected to encouragement and wisdom outside yourself so you are not doing it completely alone. You need some kind of an outside support system. The kind that helps you show up. The kind that reminds you of the *why* when you want to quit.

What's *Your* Accountability Style?

To help you pinpoint what works for you, take the quick quiz below and learn how to tailor your support system to help you achieve your financial goals.

1. **When you set a big goal, what helps you follow through?**
   A. Talking with someone who will check in with me.
   B. Being part of a group where we're all working toward the same goal.
   C. Creating a plan and tracking it myself.

2. **What sounds most motivating to you?**
   A. A trusted friend cheering me on and asking how it's going.
   B. Seeing others making progress and sharing wins together.
   C. Checking things off a list or filling in a habit tracker.

3. **When you're struggling to stay consistent, what's most helpful?**
   A. Having someone I respect remind me why I started.
   B. Knowing I'll be sharing my progress with a group.
   C. Reviewing my goals and resetting on my own.

4. **What's your ideal check-in style?**
   A. A weekly coffee date or quick text with someone I trust.
   B. A casual group chat or online community where I can pop in anytime.
   C. Quiet time to reflect, journal, or use an app.

5. **Which statement sounds most like you?**
   A. "I do best when someone is walking alongside me."
   B. "I love encouragement and energy from others."
   C. "I like doing my own thing, and I'll stay on track if I have a clear system."

Tally Your Answers:

Mostly *A*'s? You thrive with **one-on-one support.** You don't need a crowd. You just need one person who believes in you and is willing to follow up.

Mostly *B*'s? You're built for **group accountability.** You love energy, community, and the motivation that comes from working alongside others. Join (or start!) a financial challenge with others or a money goal accountability check-in group.

Mostly *C*'s? You shine with **self-accountability tools.** You're independent and motivated by structure. Use a goal tracker and/or a budgeting app, and pair that with regular check-ins with *yourself*.

How to Build Your Accountability Plan

Now that you've identified your accountability style, let's take the next step: building a plan that fits your life. The kind of plan that works with your personality, supports your goals, and makes it more likely you'll follow through, even when motivation is low.

There's no one right way to do this. You can choose just one approach, or mix and match, depending on your season or preferences. What matters most is that your plan feels doable, life-giving, and truly gives you real support.

I want it to be so rock solid that you can't help but follow through with it! That's what irresistible accountability looks like.

Irresistible accountability isn't just about choosing the right kind of support; it's also about creating a rhythm you can sustain. As much as is possible, your accountability plan should feel fairly easy and natural to stick with. It should become second nature, something that fits into your life instead of hanging over your head like another obligation on your to-do list. The more your routine feels natural and effortless, the more likely you are to keep going—especially on the hard days.

In the quiz, we broke accountability into three types: one-on-one support, group accountability, and self-accountability. Let's explore these three practical paths and how you can build a plan that works for you.

One-on-One Support

If you thrive on connection, conversation, and encouragement, one-on-one accountability can be a game-changer. This kind of support works especially well for those who do better when someone is checking in regularly, cheering them on, and helping them stay the course.

Start by choosing the right person. This could be your spouse, a trusted friend, a mentor, or even a financial coach. The key is to find someone who won't judge or shame you and who is also supportive and dependable. You want someone who believes in your growth and is willing to lovingly hold you to your plan. (If they always give you a pass when things get hard instead of helping you brainstorm ways to get back on track, they are not the best fit. You want to respect them enough that it motivates you to follow through!)

Once you've chosen someone, set clear expectations. Don't just say, "Can you help me stay on track?" Be specific. Let them know what you're working on. For instance, tell them: "I'm trying to save five hundred dollars for an emergency fund over the next three months." Then decide how and when you'll check in. Will you text a quick update every Friday? Meet for coffee once a month? Call each other at the end of every week?

You can even ask for very practical support, like: "Can you message me every Friday and ask if I stayed under my grocery budget this week?"

Finally, keep it simple and consistent. You don't need long reports. A one-line check-in is perfect. And if you mess up or miss the mark? That's okay. Talk about it. What got in the way? What could help next time?

WHERE TO FIND THE RIGHT SUPPORT

If you're not sure where to start, here are a few ideas to help you find the right person:

Look close to home. A spouse, sibling, or close friend who shares your values could be a great accountability partner.

Join a small group. Whether it's a moms' group, a church group, or a local women's meetup, chances are, someone else is working toward similar goals.

Hire a coach. If you want professional guidance, a financial coach or money mentor can offer personalized help. Most coaches offer a free discovery call to see if you're a good fit. (I highly recommend doing this.)

Post in an online community. If you're part of a budgeting group on Facebook or follow personal finance influencers, ask if anyone is looking for an accountability partner.

Ask someone you admire. Think of someone who is a little further ahead of you and living out what you're aiming for. Even if it feels intimidating, don't be afraid to reach out and ask.

When my husband and I set the goal to pay cash for our first house, we had recently moved and didn't yet have a lot of community or support. We met a family who had financial values and goals similar to ours, and they became such a strong place of accountability for us. We never had a formal accountability plan in place with them, but because we usually hung out with them at least once or twice a week, that helped spur us to continue with our goals.

We swapped ideas for saving money, we shared the best deals we found at local stores, we had freezer cooking challenges and eat-from-the-pantry challenges together, and we even had a joint family garage sale. I'm so grateful for how their family made us feel less alone in our choices and decisions. Their friendship and accountability brought such a sense of community to us during a lonely season of our lives.

Sometimes the support we need is just a conversation or connection away. Don't be afraid to ask and don't discount the power of consistent encouragement from even one person who believes in you.

Not too long ago, a young woman in our church asked me if I would be her mentor and help her with budgeting. In the months leading up to her going off to college, we met regularly to discuss how to set up a budget and then to help her stay accountable to her budget. I was so honored she would ask for my input and willingly receive it. Plus, meeting with her inspired me in my own budgeting and money-saving endeavors!

Group Accountability

Some of us are wired for community. We thrive on momentum, mutual encouragement, and the energy of others working toward the same goal. If that sounds like you, group accountability might be your sweet spot.

Start by finding (or creating) your group. This could be a Facebook group, an online forum, a small group from your church, or even just a text thread with a few like-minded friends. You can also join a formal money challenge or budgeting course that includes community support.

And if you can't find a group that fits? Start your own! Gather two to five friends who want to save, budget, or spend more intentionally, and invite them to do it *together*.

Then, choose a focus and a timeframe. Maybe it's a "Thirty-Day No-Spend Challenge" or a "Three-Month Emergency Fund Sprint." You could even keep it simple with weekly budget check-ins. Decide how often you'll connect. Will it be through daily text encouragement, a weekly Zoom, or monthly meetups? In addition, what kind of support will you offer each other?

Make it fun and motivating. Share wins and tips. Talk honestly about what's been hard. Visual trackers such as coloring charts or shared spreadsheets can add some motivation. You can even build in small group rewards like, "If we all stick to our goals this week, let's treat ourselves to a group coffee date!"

I'm part of a group accountability text thread right now made up of women I met through a business mastermind. We are all business owners, have very full lives, and live all over the country. But we check in every morning to share how we did on our goals the day before. It's amazing how much of an inspiration this is for me! When I'm tempted to make a choice that's not in line with my goals, I stop and remind myself, "You're going to need to report this to the group tomorrow. Do you really want to have to do that?" Talk about motivation!

Self-Accountability Tools

If you're more of an independent thinker (or if you love systems, quiet reflection, or creative routines) self-accountability can work beautifully. It's all about finding tools that help *you* stay focused and consistent.

First, choose tools that fit your style. Do you like to write things out? Try weekly journal prompts. Prefer visuals? Use sticky notes, goal trackers, or a whiteboard. Are you tech savvy? Set up a budgeting spreadsheet or download an app that tracks your progress. Even something simple like the paper habit tracker I mentioned previously can be a powerful motivator.

Next, create a weekly check-in rhythm. Set a time on your calendar—maybe Sunday night or Monday morning—to reflect on the week. Ask yourself questions like

- *What did I do well this week?*
- *What got in the way?*
- *What's one small adjustment I'll try next week?*

Even five minutes of honest reflection can reset your focus and keep you moving forward.

I find that a paper habit tracker in my closet right where I get dressed every day works as a great reminder for me. I keep a pen by it and check off what I accomplished the day before on my goals. This daily check-in/reminder of what I'm working toward keeps me focused and on track.

Bonus: Mix and Match for Maximum Support

You don't have to choose just one accountability method. Some of the strongest systems are layered.

While most of us have one form of accountability that is most motivating for us, I think it can be helpful to set up more than one form—just so we have covered all our bases and have some backup in place.

For instance, I find that I am usually pretty self-motivated, which is why I love to use a habit tracker or an online habit-tracking app to help me stay on task. However, I usually try to tell someone else too. That might be a friend or my husband or even posting my goals on Instagram or my blog to have an extra kick in the pants to follow through.

Mixing and matching accountability could look like

- using a budgeting spreadsheet (self-accountability),
- checking in with a friend every Friday (one-on-one support), and
- joining a thirty-day challenge online (group accountability).

Each layer adds reinforcement. So if one part slips, the others are there to help you stay on track.

Accountability Pitfalls (and How to Avoid Them)

Accountability can be a powerful tool, but only when it's the *right kind* of support. Here are a few common pitfalls to watch for and some ways around them:

Overly critical partners: Accountability should encourage, not discourage. If your partner is more focused on pointing out failures than celebrating progress, it may be time to have an honest conversation or set some new boundaries.

Reciprocal fatigue: If both you and your accountability partner are struggling, it can sometimes feel like the blind leading the blind. Don't be afraid to pause and reevaluate if your check-ins start to feel heavy or unhelpful.

Quick tips to recalibrate:

- Renegotiate how often you check in—weekly might be too much; monthly could feel more doable.
- Shift the focus of your conversations to encouragement and small wins.

- Don't be afraid to find a new partner if the dynamic just isn't working. Sometimes, a fresh start can make all the difference!

The best accountability feels like a cheerleader, not a critic. You deserve support that builds you up and helps you grow.

You're Stronger with Support

Let's just say it plainly: Building better money habits is hard when it feels like you're doing it all by yourself.

Being surrounded by people who think nothing of last-minute vacations, frequent takeout, or shopping "just because" can leave you feeling like the odd one out. Like you're behind. Like maybe you're doing something wrong.

I remember those feelings so clearly.

During the early years of our marriage, when our budget was often stretched thinner than thin, we had to be incredibly careful with every dollar we spent. That meant saying no to a lot of things, especially social events. We longed to connect with people and build friendships, but it felt like every invitation came with a price tag we couldn't afford. Most months, our entertainment category was sitting at a big fat zero.

It was discouraging. And lonely. But you know what changed things? Finding a few like-minded friends who were also living frugally.

Remember the frugal family I mentioned earlier in the chapter? They didn't just understand our choices; they were *making the same ones*. That connection made such a difference. We swapped money-saving ideas. We shared tips and resources. We celebrated each other's wins—like scoring a grocery deal or finding a secondhand treasure. Even more than that, we reminded each other that being purposeful in our financial decisions was going to be something we would benefit from for years to come!

That kind of support isn't just helpful; it's *powerful.* I look back on those years and am so grateful we weren't going it alone. Our frugal friends were a lifeline of support, camaraderie, and encouragement, and helped us to keep pressing on with our countercultural money goals!

Why Frugal Friends Make the Journey Easier

When you surround yourself with people who share your values and financial goals, everything changes:

1. **You can swap skills and stuff.**
   From babysitting trades to clothing swaps to sharing coupon strategies, frugal friends are often eager to exchange ideas and resources. It's not just practical; it's life-giving.
2. **You'll learn and grow together.**
   Some of my best frugal habits started as tips from friends—things like making homemade bread or playing the drugstore game. When you're in community, you pick up wisdom just by being in conversation.
3. **They'll cheer you on.**
   The right people will be your biggest cheerleaders. They'll celebrate your twenty-five-dollar savings win or your first month sticking to your grocery budget. And they'll remind you of your progress when you're tempted to quit.
4. **Life becomes way more fun.**
   Saving money doesn't have to feel heavy or isolating. It can joyful, especially when you're laughing with others over thrift-store finds or meal-plan victories.

Where to Find Your People

If you're thinking, *That sounds great, but I don't know anyone like that*, don't panic. Finding your frugal friends might take a little looking, but they're out there.

Try showing up in spaces where budget-conscious folks naturally gather:

- Yard sales and consignment sales
- Local libraries or community centers
- Facebook Marketplace or Buy Nothing groups
- Freecycle or swap events
- Financial Peace University classes or similar workshops
- Thrift stores, used bookstores, or pantry co-ops
- Free community events and meetups

Once you're there, don't be afraid to take the first step:

- **Start conversations.** Ask questions. Be curious. People love to share what's working for them.
- **Volunteer.** Helping out at a local sale or group can open doors to deeper connection.
- **Host something.** Invite a few friends over for a potluck, clothing swap, or no-spend game night.

Sometimes all it takes is a little courage and a message like

> "I'm working on being more intentional with my money and would love a friend to swap ideas with. Are you interested?"

And don't be afraid to think outside the box. Jesse and I once wanted to attend a party during law school, but the fee of four dollars per person didn't fit in our budget. So I emailed the host and offered to bring snacks and drinks instead (items

Frugal Friend Icebreakers

Great conversation starters to find and connect with like-minded money-savvy friends!

1. "What's your favorite way to save money on groceries?" (*Everyone has a go-to trick, and it's a great way to swap ideas!*)
2. "Have you ever done a no-spend month? How did it go?" (*This often leads to fun stories and great encouragement.*)
3. "Where's your favorite place to thrift or bargain hunt?" (*Bonus: You might end up planning a frugal friend field trip.*)
4. "What's the best deal you've scored recently?" (*Frugal friends love a good story and they'll probably ask you to share yours too.*)
5. "Are there any budget-friendly meals your family loves?" (*Great for swapping meal ideas and avoiding dinner burnout.*)
6. "Do you follow any money-saving blogs or Instagram accounts?" (*You might discover some new favorite resources.*)
7. "Have you ever made something at home instead of buying it?" (*From DIY cleaners to homemade bread, this is a great way to bond over creativity.*)
8. "Have you ever swapped stuff with friends instead of buying new?" (*Opens the door to chatting about clothing swaps, toy trades, or hand-me-downs.*)
9. "What's your favorite free thing to do in our area?" (*Perfect for discovering hidden gems in your community.*)
10. "Want to do a money challenge together sometime?" (*Whether it's a no-spend week or a hundred-dollar savings goal, inviting someone to join you builds instant accountability.*)

I had gotten almost free with coupons at the grocery store). She said yes. We had a great time, didn't spend anything, and it opened the door to additional low-cost social connections.

You Become Who You Surround Yourself With

Whether you realize it or not, the people around you shape your habits. If your environment is constantly telling you things like, "You deserve it," or "Just put it on the card," it will wear you down over time. But if you're surrounded by people who are focused on peace, purpose, and progress? Suddenly your goals don't feel so strange. They feel *normal*. Even exciting.

Ask yourself

- Who could I invite to walk with me on this journey?
- What kind of accountability rhythm would feel life-giving, not burdensome?
- How has trying to do this alone held me back?
- What's one small way I can invite support this week?

Work up your courage (even if you feel like you don't have much!) and walk through that door, send the text, start the conversation, join the class, show up at the library sale.

You don't need a dozen people. You just need a few who believe in what you're building and are willing to walk with you.

Because you're stronger with support. And your people? They might just be waiting for someone like you to go first.

You've Got This

Some people think of accountability as having a drill sergeant screaming orders in your face to motivate you to do something you don't want to do. Nope. This isn't that.

Being strategic about accountability is going to further equip you to reach the goals that you absolutely want to reach!

If you haven't built these relationships and strategies yet, let me be the first like-minded friend to cheer you on. Because, girl, if no one else has ever told you, I want you to hear it from me: I'm so proud of you and am over here with my pom-poms hollering for your success!

Journaling Prompt

Your Personal Accountability Plan: Take a few moments to think about what support would help you most. Use the prompts below to sketch your plan and make it real.

- My Goal: ______________________________
- My Preferred Style: ______________________________
- How I'll Check In (with myself or others): ______________________________
- When I'll Check In (day/time): ______________________________
- One Way I'll Celebrate Progress: ______________________________

Habit #6

Stop Paying Full Price

Shift from Passive Spender to Strategic Steward

I'll never forget the day I got paid to buy groceries—and no, it wasn't because I was DoorDashing! The store cashier actually handed me cash after scanning all the groceries I was buying because the coupons I used made my total in the negative!

Let me tell you the crazy story . . .

It was early on in our marriage, back in the golden days of couponing. Our local grocery store offered double and triple coupon days occasionally (yes, triple), which meant that on those days, the store would double or triple the value of the coupon. So on double coupon days, if the coupon was for fifty cents off, the store would take a dollar off. On triple coupon days, if the coupon was for fifty cents off, the store would take a dollar fifty off!

It was one of those double coupon days, and I had spent a solid forty-five minutes poring over the sales flyer and organizing my stack of coupons for a big grocery haul. I walked into the store armed with my carefully crafted list and my shoebox-sized Tupperware tub filled with alphabetized envelopes for different coupon categories. (What can I say? I was serious about saving money!)

I filled up my cart with the deals and pushed it confidently up to the checkout, buzzing with anticipation. After all the groceries were scanned, I handed the cashier my thick wad of coupons and watched as the total dropped lower and lower . . . until it hit zero.

But then, to my surprise, the cashier kept scanning coupons. The screen flashed a total of -$3.14.

Yes, negative.

The cashier looked at me, stunned. I was just as surprised. She called over a manager, and after a bit of back-and-forth, they opened the drawer and handed me $3.14 in cash. They *paid* me to buy groceries that day!

While couponing has changed a lot since those days, one thing hasn't: I *still* love a good deal. In fact, I've made it my mission to rarely—if ever—pay full price. In this chapter, I'm pulling back the curtain on some of my favorite secrets and strategies for stretching your dollars. We'll address the most common budget areas, and I'm going to give you a plethora of ways you can creatively save money in those areas.

Why This Habit Matters

Habit #6: Stop Paying Full Price just might be one of my favorite financial habits. Because it's where all our work and effort to be intentional with our finances gets really fun!

Scoring something you needed or wanted for 30 or 70 percent off not only feels empowering, but every dollar you don't spend unnecessarily is a dollar you can reroute toward something more meaningful: your savings goals, your giving, your future, or even just something that will bring joy to your life or someone else's.

Spending less isn't about being cheap—it's about being smart with the money you've worked so hard to earn. It's shifting from scarcity to stewardship. From "I can't afford that" to "I'm going to do the best I can with what I have!"

One important thing I want to remind you of: If you don't have a solid budget in place, there can be a real tendency to get caught up in the thrill of the hunt. Bargain shopping can become a vice of sorts when you end up "spaving"—spending money you wouldn't normally spend in an effort to "save." That's not real savings. In fact, you could actually end up spending *more* money because you feel like you don't want to miss out on an "amazing sale." (Think adding $20 of extra items to your shopping cart that you don't need, just to save $5.95 on shipping.)

I want you to hear this loud and clear: It's not a good deal for you—no matter the price—if you don't have the money in your budget.

This chapter is not encouraging you to save money on things you don't need or to become someone who is constantly going from store to store, garage sale to garage sale, loading up on discounted treasures just because "it was a good deal." That kind of spending, even if the price tags are small, adds up quickly and often leads to more clutter, less clarity, and greater financial burden.

Instead, I want to invite you to a mindset shift from being a passive spender to becoming a strategic steward.

When you shift from asking, *Can I afford this?* to *Is this aligned with my priorities, values, and goals?* everything changes. You're no longer just reacting to sales and price tags. You're proactively aligning your spending with what matters most to you.

This is where the first five habits we've talked about in this book come into play. These habits help you put the right guardrails in place so the money you save by being thoughtful in your spending and looking for ways to not pay full price actually moves the needle in your budget and contributes to your greater financial health.

It's not about hoarding or hustling; it's about intentionality.

That means planning ahead and being patient. Sometimes the best deals are found not in the clearance aisle but in the clarity of knowing what you truly need and waiting for the right time to purchase it.

Occasionally, when I talk about how much I love finding great deals, people respond with resistance, telling me that they don't want to be cheap or they feel guilty paying less than full price if they can afford to pay full price.

Let's reframe the narrative: Looking for great deals doesn't make you cheap or stingy—it makes you wise. You're refusing to assume that full price is your only option. You're training yourself to pause and ask, *Is there a better way?* and often, there is.

There's a deep joy that comes from waiting, watching, and winning . . . not in a frantic or obsessive way, but in a peaceful, purposeful one. When you wait for the right time and the right price, you're not just saving money, you're practicing discipline, building confidence, and reinforcing your values.

Grocery and Household Staples: Where Overspending Adds Up Fast

For many families, the food budget is the largest flexible monthly expense. Unlike your rent or mortgage, groceries are one of the few areas you can adjust week by week to create breathing room in your budget. But without a plan, it's also one of the easiest places to overspend.

The good news? There are so many simple, doable strategies that can help you stop paying full price, without sacrificing quality or nutrition. I could write a whole book on strategies to save money on groceries (we have well over a hundred articles on MoneySavingMom.com with more ideas plus years of frugal recipes and menu plans), but I'll condense things down to some of my best suggestions in this chapter.

1. Plan Your Meals Around What's on Sale

Instead of creating a meal plan based on cravings or ideas you find online, flip your strategy. Look at your local store's weekly sales ad and build your meals around what's marked down. You'll stretch your dollars further and reduce food waste by focusing on what's already discounted.

BUILD YOUR MENU AROUND THE BEST DEALS ON . . .

1. **Whole chicken:** Roast it for Sunday dinner, then use leftovers for chicken soup, quesadillas, or fried rice.
2. **Canned tomatoes or pasta sauce:** Plan baked ziti, lasagna, or skillet pasta with whatever protein is on sale.
3. **Sweet potatoes:** Make loaded sweet potatoes with black beans, BBQ chicken, or taco filling.
4. **Frozen veggies:** Use for stir-fry, quick soups, or throw into scrambled eggs and rice bowls.
5. **Pork loin:** Make pulled pork sandwiches, roast with veggies, or slice for stir-fry.
6. **Salmon or other fish:** Try baked lemon-garlic salmon, fish tacos, or a simple sheet-pan fish and veggies.
7. **Rotisserie chicken:** Use it for chicken salad, enchiladas, or toss into soup or pasta.
8. **Ground turkey:** Plan for turkey chili, lettuce wraps, or stuffed peppers.

9. **Italian sausage:** Cook up sausage and peppers, toss in pasta, or make sausage breakfast burritos.
10. **Eggs:** Serve breakfast for dinner, make quiche, or prep hard-boiled eggs for lunches.
11. **Bell peppers:** Make fajitas, stuffed peppers, or dice and freeze for omelets and soups.
12. **Cabbage:** Plan egg roll in a bowl, coleslaw, or cabbage stir-fry.
13. **Apples or pears:** Bake into crisps, slice into salads, or simmer into homemade applesauce.
14. **Tortillas:** Plan quesadillas, burritos, wraps, or make-your-own pizza night.
15. **Cheese:** Shred and freeze, plan grilled-cheese night, or add to casseroles.

2. Use Online Resources to Menu Plan

Not sure what to make with items that are on sale at your store? Do a quick Google search or go to ChatGPT and type in the ingredients and ask for recipe ideas. For instance, "Chicken, pork loin, bell peppers, cheese, and pasta are on sale at my store this week. Give me 15 meal ideas that are inexpensive that I can make using some or all of these ingredients."

Here's what ChatGPT gave me with that prompt:

15 INEXPENSIVE MEAL IDEAS BASED ON WHAT'S ON SALE

1. **Sheet-Pan Chicken Fajitas**
   Sliced chicken + bell peppers + onions + taco seasoning. Bake and serve with tortillas or rice.
2. **Cheesy Chicken Pasta Bake**
   Cooked pasta + shredded chicken + cheese + jarred sauce or cream. Bake until bubbly.

3. **Pork Stir-Fry**
   Thin-sliced pork loin + bell peppers + soy sauce + garlic. Serve over rice or noodles.
4. **Bell Pepper and Cheese Omelets**
   Great meatless option or add diced chicken or pork leftovers. Serve with toast or roasted potatoes.
5. **BBQ Pork Sliders with Bell Pepper Slaw**
   Slow cook pork loin in barbeque sauce. Shred and serve on buns with a crunchy pepper slaw.
6. **Chicken Alfredo Pasta**
   Cooked pasta + sautéed chicken + homemade or jarred Alfredo sauce + cheese on top.
7. **Pork & Pepper Quesadillas**
   Sauté diced pork + peppers + cheese in tortillas. Crisp these in a skillet and slice.
8. **Baked Ziti with Chicken**
   Pasta + marinara + chunks of chicken + mozzarella or Italian cheese blend. Bake and serve with garlic bread.
9. **Cheesy Stuffed Bell Peppers**
   Halve peppers and fill with cooked rice + shredded chicken or pork + cheese. Bake until tender.
10. **Creamy One-Pot Chicken & Pasta Skillet**
    Cook chicken and pasta in one pan with broth and milk, then stir in cheese and diced peppers.

You can take this list and choose four or five of the recipes to make this week. To save even more, you can repeat this process using some ingredients you already have on hand.

3. Shop (and Stock Up on!) the Loss Leaders

Loss leaders are the items stores price extra-low to get you in the door. The store is taking a loss on those products when you buy them. They are hoping the good deals will lure you in the door and then you'll buy those plus load up your cart with a lot of other items that they'll make money on.

Think $1.99 for a pound of strawberries or $5.95 for a rotisserie chicken. These are often featured on the front page of the store's weekly ad and can be the foundation of your weekly meal plan if you stay flexible and creative.

Instead of just adding a few of these to your cart, plan your menu around them (as we just explored) and stock up on as much of them as you can or will use in the next two to twelve weeks, depending upon whether it's a shelf-stable item or can be frozen. Most stores have six- to twelve-week sales cycles, meaning most items go on sale every six to twelve weeks. If you stock up when items are at their lowest prices and buy enough to last until the next sale, you'll significantly cut your grocery bill because you will rarely be paying full price for items.

There are price tracker apps or printable sheets or spreadsheets you can download to track what the best prices are, but in the beginning, if you aren't sure if something is a good deal, my rule of thumb is that if it's something you regularly buy and use and it's at least 40 percent off, that's a good deal for you. Over time, as you pay more attention to prices, you'll have a better gauge of what is a great deal for your store and when things are at their lowest prices, but the 40 percent off marker is a good place to start!

▸ **Tip: Create a "Buy-Price List"**

If you don't want to download an app or set up a spreadsheet, I recommend at least keeping a simple list (either in your notes app on your phone or in a small notebook) of what a good deal looks like for your favorite products. For example, you might jot down: "Cereal: Buy at $1.99 a box or less" or "Ground beef: Stock up at $4.99 a pound or less" This keeps you from second-guessing in the store and helps you know whether it's time to stock up or wait for a better deal.

4. Shop Your Pantry Before Making Your Grocery List

Over the years, I've learned to plan our meals around what we already have. I've dubbed this strategy *Reverse Meal-Planning*. Instead of starting with recipes and shopping for the ingredients, I start with what's already in my kitchen and build meals from there.

It's not complicated! In fact, I've narrowed it down to my simple *ABC*'s of **Reverse Meal-Planning**:

Assess What You Have

Before you can use it, you need to see it. Take ten to fifteen minutes to scan your pantry, fridge, and freezer. Toss anything expired or freezer-burned. Then group what's left by category—meats, veggies, grains, canned goods, etc. This makes it so much easier to spot potential meals at a glance.

To stay on top of it, jot down a quick inventory on a whiteboard or notepad. That way, you're not buying duplicates and you'll be reminded to use what you already have.

Break the Rules

There are no "right" combinations. If your pantry says taco night and your freezer says broccoli, go with it and do both! Some of our favorite meals have come from odd pairings that just *worked*. It doesn't have to be impressive. If your family likes it, that's what matters.

The same goes for sides. If apples and carrots are the produce on sale this week, serve them with multiple meals. You'll save money and reduce waste. Plus, over time, you'll naturally rotate in a variety of foods.

Create New Recipes

If a recipe calls for something you don't have, try a simple swap! Don't have ground beef? Use shredded pork. Out of white rice? Try quinoa or brown rice. Many recipes are more flexible than we think.

Start small and give yourself permission to experiment. Some dinners may flop, but others will become new family favorites. And remember, most things are fixable with a little extra cheese or a scoop of ice cream!

"Plug and Play" Meal Framework—Creative Theme Night Ideas

Want to simplify menu planning? Having theme nights for your menu can streamline the planning process and make it easy to get dinner on the table every night. Plus, you can plan around your schedule (for instance, if you always have youth group on Wednesday nights, you can pick a theme that is super quick so you can get out the door on time).

Here are some ideas to get you started:

Meatless Monday

Use sale-priced beans, lentils, eggs, or veggies.

Ideas: Black bean tacos, veggie stir-fry, lentil soup, or breakfast for dinner

Build-a-Bowl Night

Base: Rice, quinoa, greens, noodles, or couscous

Toppings: Whatever protein and produce is on sale

Ideas: Burrito bowls, Mediterranean bowls, Asian noodle bowls

Casserole Night

Combine protein + carb + veggie + sauce/cheese

Ideas: Chicken-and-rice bake, tuna noodle casserole, or shepherd's pie

Soup & Sandwich Night

Make soup from clearance produce or pantry items and sandwiches with whatever deli meat or cheese is on sale

Ideas: Tomato soup with grilled cheese, chicken soup with paninis

DIY Pizza Night

Use whatever base is cheapest—flatbread, naan, English muffins, tortillas—and let everyone top with what's in the fridge (cheese, leftovers, veggies)

Salad Bar Night

Use markdown produce, leftover meat, hard-boiled eggs, canned beans

Ideas: Cobb salad, taco salad, or "clean out the fridge" chopped salad

Baked Potato Bar

Load up baked potatoes or sweet potatoes with cheese, chili, or sautéed veggies. This is perfect for using up bits of leftovers or sale toppings

International Night

Choose a different cuisine each week based on sales.

Ideas: Stir-fry (Asian), enchiladas (Mexican), curry (Indian), pasta (Italian)

Breakfast-for-Dinner Night

Make pancakes and eggs, French toast and bacon, or even a breakfast casserole or omelets.

▸ Tip: Make the Most of Leftovers

Instead of seeing leftovers as boring, view them as an opportunity to innovate. Transform last night's dinner into a completely new meal. Leftover roasted chicken can become chicken tacos, a hearty soup, or a homemade pizza topping. Stale bread? Turn it into croutons or bread pudding.

A weekly "Leftover Night" can also be a great way to reduce waste and give yourself a break from cooking an entirely new meal. We plan Leftover Night into our menu rotation. I just set out all the odds and ends from the fridge and people can make their plates up based upon what they are hungry for. It means we use up a lot more of what we have, and I don't have to cook or do many dishes that night.

5. Use Cash-Back Apps (Like Ibotta, Fetch, Shopkick, and Receipt Hog)

These free apps reward you with points or cash back for scanning receipts or purchasing certain items. Ibotta and Fetch are two of my favorites. If you're already buying milk or eggs or bread, why not earn a little money back? It's digital couponing without the scissors.

▸ **Tip: Don't Skip the Digital Coupons and Store Apps**

Most grocery stores have apps that allow you to "clip" digital coupons and load them directly to your loyalty card. These add up fast, especially on staples like produce, dairy, and pantry items. Bonus: Some stores even offer personalized coupons based on what you buy most often.

6. Simplify Your Ingredients

A fancy recipe with fifteen specialty ingredients might look amazing online, but it can quickly eat up your grocery budget and leave you with half-used jars sitting in your fridge. Instead, aim for meals built around simple, affordable staples you already know and love like rice, beans, eggs, potatoes, seasonal produce, pasta, and budget-friendly meats.

Start noticing what ingredients you tend to buy regularly, and plan meals around those. If you always have tortillas, shredded cheese, and a few cans of beans on hand, tacos, quesadillas, or burrito bowls can be an easy go-to. If fresh herbs often go bad before you use them up, consider switching to dried, freezing the extras, or growing a small herb pot by the kitchen window.

Also, make it a habit to *rescue ingredients before they go to waste*. If you opened a jar of pasta sauce or used half a can of coconut milk, try to plan a second recipe later in the week to use the rest. You can even pop extra broth, tomato paste, or herbs into ice cube trays and freeze them for future use.

And if you're stumped for ideas? Just search:

"I have a lot of [insert ingredient]. What are some simple meals I can make with it?"

Seriously, as I mentioned earlier, Google or ChatGPT can be your best friend when it comes to finding easy, budget-friendly ways to use what you have.

Keeping meals simple doesn't mean being boring; it means being smart. Fewer ingredients, less waste, and more money saved. Win-win-win.

Clothing and Shoes: Dressing for Less Without Sacrificing Style

Looking great and feeling confident in what you wear doesn't have to break your budget. In fact, some of the best wardrobes aren't built by spending more but by creatively shopping smart and embracing what I call *intentional frugality*.

Let's talk about how to clothe your family (and yourself) on a budget without sacrificing style or quality.

How to Shop Clearance and Off-Season Like a Pro

One of my all-time favorite strategies? Buying clothing **at the end of the season for the following year**. This means scooping up summer items in late August or snagging winter gear in February or March, when retailers are desperate to clear out inventory. I've found jackets for my kids at 70 to 90 percent off just by shopping off-season!

To take your savings to the next level, get to know the ins and outs of your favorite store's clearance schedule. Many stores follow a predictable cycle—some restock and mark down items on specific days of the week, while others move inventory to final clearance after a set period. Learning when new markdowns happen or how long items typically stay on clearance can help you time your shopping for maximum discounts.

And don't be shy about chatting with a store associate. They often know when major sales are coming or when a big batch of clearance is about to hit the floor. A little insider knowledge can help you build next season's wardrobe for a fraction of the typical cost.

When shopping clearance, here's what helps:

- **Have a running list.** Know what sizes and items you're looking for. That way, when you come across a sale, you can quickly check to see if there's anything that meets a need.
- **Don't buy just because it's cheap.** A $3 shirt you never wear isn't a bargain.
- **Think ahead.** If your child is in a size six now, consider buying size seven or eight for next year's cold weather.

Over time, you'll build up a small stash of clothes bought on major markdown, and you'll rarely need to pay full price again.

Why Buying Used Isn't Second-Best—It's Often Better!

Buying secondhand is wise, resourceful, and often allows you to get great deals on higher-quality items that will last.

FAVORITE SECONDHAND SOURCES

- **Thrift stores:** Take a few minutes to browse your local thrift shops. Many have weekly color tag sales where all items that have a certain tag color are discounted, so you can save off the already-discounted price.

- **Host a Swap Night:** Have everyone bring items they were planning to donate—clothes, toys, books, or whatever parameters you decide—and make trades.
- **Consignment sales/events:** These seasonal pop-ups are goldmines for gently used kids' clothes, shoes, and gear. I prefer these to shopping at thrift stores because I find that there's usually a lot more selection so it can save a lot of time.
- **A friend:** If you have a friend who has a child older than yours and would be willing to hand down their clothes, this can be the perfect way to outfit kids for less. Offer to pay for the clothes and it could end up being a blessing to both of you: She doesn't have to haul them to donate and makes a little money, and you don't have to go searching for clothes and deals—and you save money!
- **Online resale sites:**
  - **ThredUp:** Especially great for women's and kids' clothing. Watch for 50 percent off sales or first-time user discounts. You do want to pay close attention to pricing because some things aren't really a great deal.
  - **Poshmark:** Search by brand, size, and condition. You can also make offers! I highly recommend this site if you are looking for a specific brand/make in a certain size. We bought Kaitlynn's senior prom dress that had only been worn once at a *huge* discount from this site. I've also bought name-brand jeans for significantly less.
  - **eBay:** A treasure trove for name-brand shoes, coats, and specific items (think soccer cleats, formalwear, school uniforms).

▸ **Tip:** When shopping online secondhand, **filter by "new with tags" or "like new"** if that's important to you. Many items have barely been worn—or not worn at all!

When to Splurge, When to Save (and How to Save Even on the Splurges)

Sometimes, it *is* worth spending a little more on items like

- Well-made jeans that fit you like a glove
- Durable winter boots
- A classic black dress you'll wear to weddings, funerals, or special events
- A great pair of sneakers if you're on your feet a lot

Even then, you don't have to pay full price. Here are some ways to save on splurge-worthy items:

- **Sign up for emails to get a first-time discount.** Many sites offer coupon codes and discounts if you sign up for their email list or text offers.
- **Search online for cash back and coupon codes.** Before you purchase anything online, always search online to see if there are cash back options and/or coupon codes. Sites like Rakuten offer a percentage of cash back when you click through their site to purchase (this adds up over time, even if you don't shop online much!) and also search online for a coupon code (Google the store name + coupon code) you can use at checkout. My philosophy is that if it takes 2 minutes to search for cash back and coupon code options and it saves you a few dollars, that's definitely worth your time!
- **Wait for major sales events like Black Friday/Cyber Monday, Memorial Day, or Back to School.** If you're planning

a big purchase or want to refresh your wardrobe, it's smart to time your shopping around these events. You can also add items to your online shopping cart ahead of time and wait to see if prices drop during a sale.

Gifts, Holidays, and Celebrations: Meaningful Without the Markup

It's easy to feel that showing love and making memories means spending a lot of money. The good news? You can create meaningful moments and give thoughtful gifts without blowing your budget or sacrificing joy. The key is intentionality. Let's talk about how to celebrate well without the overwhelm (or the overspending).

Why Planning Ahead Is Your Secret Weapon

One of the most powerful tools for stress-free (and budget-friendly) giving is planning ahead. When you're not rushing to grab something last minute, you give yourself the gift of time—to shop smarter, think creatively, and stretch your dollars further.

Planning ahead allows you to

- Shop sales instead of paying full price
- Spread out the expense over several months
- Personalize gifts more thoughtfully
- Avoid the last-minute "gift guilt" that leads to overspending

The Magic of Gift Closets + Year-Round Deal Hunting

Want to make holidays, birthdays, teacher gifts, and baby showers so much easier? Create a gift closet (or bin, or shelf)! This is a stash of new, unused items you've picked up on clearance, during off-season sales, or with great coupons and have ready to go when the occasion calls.

Here's how to start:

- **Set aside a monthly budget amount** so you're not scrambling to figure out how to pay for gifts.
- **Look for 70 to 90 percent off clearance items after holidays** (toys after Christmas, candles and fancier chocolate after Valentine's Day, pretty hand towels after Mother's Day) that would be great for birthdays and special occasions when you want to bring a gift. Purchase what you can from your gift budget that month.
- **Keep a running list of upcoming gift needs** (friends' and family birthdays, baby showers, holidays) and look for sales on them.
- When you find a great deal on an item that would be a great baby shower gift or birthday gift or graduation gift, **buy extras to keep in your gift closet.**
- **Include gift wrap, tags, or bags in your stash**—all bought on clearance!
- **Regularly check to see what you have in your gift closet** and pay attention to what you are running low on so you can stock up when you find another great deal.

Using Coupons, Cash Back, and Rewards Points to Buy Gifts

Just as you can save on groceries and clothes, you can also save big on gift giving when you get strategic.

- **Coupons:** Look for store or manufacturer coupons around key gift seasons (Mother's Day, Black Friday/Cyber Monday, graduation time). I usually just search online for the site I'm planning to shop through with the phrase *coupon code* and see what comes up!

- **Rewards points:** Redeem drugstore points (like Walgreens Balance Rewards or CVS ExtraCare bucks), cash back you have accumulated from shopping online throughout the year through a cash-back site like Rakuten, grocery fuel points for discounted gift cards, or store credit you can use for gifts.

I've often used gift cards earned through rewards or cash-back apps to cover Christmas gifts or birthday presents without even touching our main budget! I save up all year and then cash them in at Christmas time.

Frugal Traditions Our Family Has Loved

The most meaningful memories often cost very little. Here are a few traditions we've treasured over the years:

- **Homemade Gifts:** We've made everything from sugar scrubs, homemade treats, hot cocoa or cookie mixes in jars to hand-stamped bookmarks and photo magnets or mugs. These are especially great for grandparents and neighbors.
- **Memory-Based Gifts:** One year, I created photo albums for grandparents with pictures of our kids from the past year. It was fun and special to do! Growing up, my parents gave all our relatives a "subscription" to a monthly newsletter they would create, print out, and mail to them. The extended family *loved* it, and it was so meaningful. We still have all the issues from those newsletters and it's wonderful to go back through and read them.
- **Experience-Based Celebrations:** Instead of giving a lot of gifts, consider experiences instead.

- **Put together a coupon book** for special one-on-one time or offering to do tasks for the person (like washing their car) that they don't enjoy—I've given this multiple times!
- **Make a movie-night gift basket.** A relative made this for our kids, and it was so much fun! She included movie theater candy, bags of microwave popcorn, and codes so they could go online and choose a movie to rent.
- **Create a book of favorite family recipes.** A family member once made and gifted us one of these, and it's been a well-used part of our kitchen.

These experiences cost little but create connection and lasting, meaningful memories. When you plan ahead, shop with intention, and focus on what matters most, you'll find that the pressure lifts and the enjoyment multiplies. You don't have to spend a lot to give a lot. Sometimes, the most memorable gifts are the ones money could never buy.

▸ **Tip:** Looking for more ideas? Visit MoneySavingMom.com/ChristmasBudget/ for a free list of creative ways to fund your Christmas budget in just fifteen minutes a day.

Homemade Christmas Gift Ideas

1. **Holiday Spice Sugar Scrub**
   A cozy, pampering gift made with basic pantry ingredients like sugar, coconut oil, and cinnamon or clove essential oils. Spoon into small mason jars and tie with a ribbon and tag—perfect for teachers, neighbors, or friends.
2. **Christmas Potpourri (Frugal or Fancy!)**
   Combine dried oranges, cinnamon sticks, whole cloves, and cranberries in a clear bag with a festive tag that reads, "Simmer

for a house that smells like Christmas." Add greenery or essential oils to elevate it.

3. **Recipe Box or Book**
   Handwrite or type up your favorite family recipes and place them in a decorated recipe box or small scrapbook. This gift feels deeply personal and is especially thoughtful for adult children, newlyweds, and close friends.
4. **Tile Coasters**
   Make custom coasters using plain ceramic tiles, Mod Podge, and printed photos or scrapbook paper. Seal with clear spray and stick felt pads on the bottom. These look professionally made and are super easy!
5. **Pressed Flower Bookmarks**
   Gather flowers or leaves, press them in a heavy book, and attach to cardstock with glue and then laminate. These are lovely tucked into a book or as a standalone token of encouragement or appreciation.
6. **Homemade Cinnamon Rolls**
   Bake a batch of your favorite cinnamon rolls and deliver them in a disposable baking tin or wrapped in parchment paper and twine. Include a note: "For a sweet start to Christmas morning!"
7. **Hot Chocolate Card Kit**
   Tuck hot cocoa packets, mini marshmallows, and candy canes into a cute mug or cellophane bag, then attach a card that says, "You're the marshmallow to my cocoa." Great for group gifting!
8. **"Reasons I Love You" Jar**
   Fill a jar with small slips of paper listing things you love, appreciate, or admire about the recipient. This gift is emotionally rich and unforgettable and perfect for spouses, parents, grandparents, and kids.
9. **Homemade Granola**
   Whip up a batch of homemade granola (with festive add-ins like cranberries or cinnamon) and package it in a mason jar or brown paper bag. Add a handwritten label for a delicious, heartfelt gift.

10. **Lemon Kitchen Hand Scrub**
    Mix sugar, coconut oil, and lemon juice or zest for a bright, grease-cutting scrub that's perfect for home cooks. Package in a jar with a ribbon and a little tag. It's both pretty and practical!
11. **DIY Sharpie Mugs**
    Buy plain white mugs and use oil-based Sharpie markers to create personalized designs or hand-lettered messages. Bake at 350 degrees for thirty minutes to help the design set. These are great paired with cocoa or coffee packets.
12. **Rice-Filled Heating/Cooling Packs**
    Sew simple rectangular pouches and fill with rice and dried lavender or essential oils. These can be microwaved or frozen and are wonderful for aches, tension, or providing winter warmth. A practical and comforting gift.
13. **Baking Mixes in a Jar**
    Layer dry ingredients for cookies, brownies, or pancakes in a clear jar, and attach a tag with baking instructions. These look beautiful and are perfect for busy moms or anyone who loves freshly baked treats.
14. **Personalized Towel**
    Use iron-on vinyl, fabric paint, or embroidery to personalize hand towels with names, holiday designs, or monograms. A thoughtful gift for grandparents, newlyweds, or friends in a new home.
15. **Freezer Meals**
    Prepare and freeze a favorite dinner (soup, casserole, or breakfast burritos), and gift it with a note that says, "A night off from cooking on me." This is especially appreciated by new moms, caregivers, or anyone going through a tough season.

Dollar Tree Stocking-Stuffer Ideas

For Kids

- **Mini puzzles or board games**—Compact and fun options like checkers or matching games.
- **Play-Doh or modeling clay**—Great for creativity and mess-free fun.
- **Stickers or sticker books**—Always a hit with little ones.
- **Coloring books and crayons**—Pair together for a quick creative set for just a few dollars.
- **Character toothbrushes**—Fun *and* practical!
- **Glow sticks or bracelets**—Perfect for winter nights or just for fun.
- **Bouncy balls**—Small and super entertaining.
- **Bubble bath or bath bombs**—Often found with fun themes or scents.
- **Novelty socks**—Kids' sizes with prints like dinosaurs or unicorns.
- **Slime or putty**—Great sensory toy (just be sure you're okay with goo!).

For Teens and Tweens

- **Lip balm or gloss**—Name-brand or flavored options.
- **Nail polish or nail art kits**—Great selection for DIY manis.
- **Mini journals or notepads**—For reminders, doodles, or lists.
- **Phone grip stands or cases**— They often have stylish ones available!
- **Earbuds**—Basic but useful stocking add-in.
- **Hair accessories**—Scrunchies, headbands, or clips.
- **Mini mirrors or makeup brushes**—Cute and functional.
- **Socks**—Fun prints or cozy fuzzy styles.

For Men

- **Travel-sized grooming products**—Razors, shave cream, or deodorant.

- **Keychains or car air fresheners**—Always handy and often themed.
- **Mini flashlights**—Great for glove boxes or tool kits.
- **Shoe polish kits**—A practical mini gift.
- **Socks**—Yes, even guys appreciate new socks!
- **Puzzle books**—Crossword, Sudoku, or word searches.

For Women

- **Face masks or spa items**—Sheet masks, bath salts, or scrubs.
- **Scented candles**—Small but lovely gift options.
- **Stationery items**—Pretty pens, sticky notes, or notepads.
- **Mugs**—Often surprisingly cute or inspirational.
- **Cosmetic bags**—Great for organizing purses or travel items.

Food & Treats (for everyone!)

- **Hot chocolate packets**—Add marshmallows or a candy cane.
- **Mini candy boxes**—Name brands in stocking-friendly sizes.
- **Gum or mints**—Always useful.
- **Trail mix or mini snack bags**—Healthy(ish) and easy to fit in.
- **Popcorn balls or holiday-themed treats**—Fun festive add-ons.

Subscriptions, Streaming, and Tech: Sneaky Budget Leaks

Do you have money seeping out of your budget without your realizing it? It's amazing how easy it is to subscribe to things and then completely forget that you did!

- Audit your recurring payments—often people are paying full price and don't realize it.
- Tips for cutting or negotiating:

- Use Trim, Rocket Money, or manual review
- Downgrade plans or share accounts
- Take advantage of free trials strategically (and make sure to cancel!)

- Switch to annual billing or promotional rates when it saves money long-term.

Travel, Experiences, and Entertainment: Yes, You Can Save Here Too!

It's a common myth that travel and entertainment are luxuries available only to people with big bank accounts. But here's the truth: You *can* enjoy memorable experiences—vacations, date nights, family outings, and even bigger trips—*without* going into debt or draining your savings.

It just takes creativity, some planning ahead, and a commitment to thoughtful spending.

Booking Smarter: Flexibility Is Your Secret Weapon

One of the easiest ways to save on travel is by staying flexible.

- **Travel on off-peak days:** Flights and hotel stays are often cheaper on Tuesdays, Wednesdays, and Saturdays. Avoiding holidays and peak travel weekends can shave hundreds off your total cost.
- **Go off-season:** Visit popular destinations in the "shoulder season" (right before or after the peak). You'll find smaller crowds and lower prices. Think early May instead of July, or mid-September instead of late December.
- **Track prices:** Use tools like Google Flights, Hopper, or Kayak's "Price Alert" feature to monitor and book when prices dip.

It's not about cutting corners; it's about traveling smart.

Local Fun for Less

Travel doesn't have to mean getting on a plane. There's often *so much* to explore right in your own city or state, especially when you're intentional about seeking out low-cost or free options.

- **Museum memberships:** A one-time fee often pays for itself in just a few visits—and many offer reciprocal benefits in other cities.
- **Library perks:** Beyond books, many libraries offer free family passes to local attractions, discounted tickets, or streaming movie subscriptions.
- **Local deal sites:** Groupon, LivingSocial, or city-specific apps often feature discounts on concerts, events, classes, restaurants, and more.
- **Parks and trails:** Explore state parks, hiking trails, or nature preserves—many are free or just a few dollars per vehicle.
- **Free community events:** Keep an eye on your city's calendar for festivals, parades, outdoor movies, and summer concert series.

With a little digging, you'll discover that fun doesn't have to cost a fortune.

Staying on Budget for Vacations

One of the best ways to avoid post-vacation financial regret is to set a clear spending cap *before* you start planning. Then, find creative ways to stick to it.

Here are a few of our favorite strategies:

- **Book accommodations with kitchens** to save on dining out (hello, easy breakfasts and picnic lunches!).
- **Plan one splurge and keep the rest simple.** Maybe it's a nice dinner out or an amusement park visit—balance it with free or low-cost activities on other days.
- **Give your kids (and/or yourself) a souvenir budget.** It keeps spending in check and makes choices more meaningful.
- **Use cash envelopes** for food, gas, and entertainment. It's a great way to stay mindful of your spending in the moment.

Vacations shouldn't leave you stressed. When you plan with purpose, you get the fun without the financial hangover.

Real Story: Our Trip to Iceland

Back in 2018, we wanted to take our three older kids on an international trip over the summer. We were hoping to go somewhere in Europe. However, when we priced airfare, it was going to be so expensive to fly to any of the main tourist locations (Rome, Paris, London, etc.) that we decided to think outside the box. We looked at any European country that had really great airline prices . . . and Iceland was what we came up with. They were offering tickets at a steal!

I cashed in some Hotels.com gift cards, and we used those to book an Airbnb we found a great deal on. (When we got there, we discovered it was over a local bar, so no wonder it was priced so affordably. However, we never felt unsafe, and it made for great people-watching!) We planned to visit locations that were mostly free and we decided to walk everywhere, except for the day we took a bus tour, which we also got a crazy-good deal on with a Groupon voucher.

I researched and discovered that food was quite expensive in Iceland. Not to be deterred, we ended up bringing a whole bunch of prepackaged food in our checked luggage (since we got one free checked bag per person) and then once we arrived in Iceland, we went to the discount grocery store to buy some things.

We ended up eating out only a few times—at Subway, at a hot dog stand, and while we were on the bus tour. Otherwise, we made everything in our little Airbnb kitchen or ate packaged food. By the end, we were very tired of granola bars and meat sticks, but we'd had an amazing trip and experienced all sorts of incredible things—and we'd done it on a very small budget.

Big Purchases and Bills: When Saving 10 Percent Means Hundreds Back in Your Pocket

When it comes to saving money, it's easy to focus on small daily decisions, and those *do* add up. But some of the biggest wins come from being strategic with your *big expenses*. Whether it's replacing an appliance, paying a medical bill, or renewing your car insurance, even a 10 percent savings can mean serious money back in your pocket.

Let's talk about how to approach those bigger bills and purchases with a money-saving mindset.

Appliances, Furniture, and Electronics: Time It Right + Shop Smart

Big-ticket items like washers, couches, and laptops often have predictable sales cycles. If you can wait, **timing your purchase** can mean major discounts.

Here's how to save big:

- **Shop holiday weekends:** Black Friday/Cyber Monday, Labor Day, and Memorial Day are goldmines for appliance and electronics deals.

- **Buy last year's model:** When a new version comes out, retailers often mark down the previous model—even though it still works great.
- **Ask for price matching:** Stores like Walmart, Best Buy, and Home Depot will sometimes match a lower advertised price even after your purchase if you see a better deal within a certain window.
- **Look for scratch-and-dent deals:** These items are often discounted 30 to 50 percent for minor cosmetic flaws that don't affect function.
- **Use cash-back sites and apps:** Before buying online, check Rakuten, Capital One Shopping, or Honey for coupons and cash back.

▸ **Tip:** If you're buying online, try adding the item to your cart and waiting a few days. Retailers often send a discount code to encourage you to finish your purchase!

Medical Bills: Don't Just Pay—Ask Questions First

Medical expenses can feel overwhelming, but you may have *more power than you think.*

Here are a few ways to make them more manageable:

- **Ask for a discount for paying in cash.** Many providers offer 10 to 30 percent off just for skipping the paperwork of insurance billing.
- **Request an itemized bill.** This allows you to check for duplicate charges or mistakes—which are surprisingly common.
- **Negotiate a payment plan.** Most offices will work with you to spread out your bill over several months or more without interest.

- **Ask about financial assistance.** Hospitals and larger providers often have programs—even for middle-income families—that can reduce or forgive balances.

▸ **Tip:** If you get a bill that feels too high, don't panic. Call and say, "Is there anything you can do to reduce this?" You'd be amazed how often the answer is yes.

Auto and Home Insurance: Don't Set It and Forget It

Insurance premiums creep up over time but you don't have to just accept it.

Every year or two, make it a habit to

- **Shop around.** Compare quotes from at least three to five providers (many websites make this quick and easy).
- **Ask about bundling.** You can often save 10 to 20 percent by purchasing home and auto insurance from the same company.
- **Request discounts.** Some common ones include:
  - Good driver
  - Low mileage
  - Safe vehicle
  - Loyalty
  - Paperless billing or autopay
- **Increase your deductible.** If you have a solid emergency fund, raising your deductible can lower your monthly premium.

▸ **Tip:** We've saved hundreds of dollars a year just by calling and saying, "I'm thinking of switching providers—are there any discounts or changes you can offer?"

Utilities and Cell Phone Plans: Negotiate, Switch, or Streamline

These monthly bills can feel fixed—but they're often negotiable or at least *optimizable.*

Ideas to save:

- **Call your provider and ask for a better rate.** It helps to say, "I'm comparing plans. Can you match this competitor's offer?"
- **Cut unused features.** Review your phone and cable bills for subscriptions, fees, or services you don't need.
- **Switch carriers.** Mobile Virtual Network Operators (MVNOs like Mint Mobile, Visible, or Consumer Cellular) often offer drastically lower cell phone plans—sometimes as low as $15 a month.
- **Install energy-saving devices.** A programmable thermostat, low-flow showerhead, or LED bulbs can lower your utility bills over time.
- **Sign up for budget billing or energy-saving rebates.** Many utility companies offer free assessments, off-peak rate programs, or even cash-back incentives for reducing usage.

These aren't changes you'll need to make every month. Reviewing just a few of these areas once or twice a year can add up to hundreds (or even thousands) of dollars saved with very little ongoing effort.

When you approach big expenses with intention instead of on autopilot, you step into the role of a wise steward—saving not just cents, but real financial margin for what matters most.

Where There's a Will, There's Often a Creative Way

When my husband and I were first married, we wanted to have internet service, but we didn't have any money in the budget to pay for it. For the first year, we used the free ten hours a month offered by JUNO. (Anyone fondly recall having an @juno.com email address like I did?) We were really careful with what we used the internet for and would make those ten hours last for the whole month.

As I started doing more online to earn money (mystery shopping, taking surveys, and starting my own online business), ten hours a month was no longer cutting it. A friend of ours told us how to get free internet from America Online (remember AOL?). AOL would send discs in the mail offering free internet access for thirty days. At the end of thirty days, if you didn't cancel, you would be charged their full fee. However, if you called to cancel on the twenty-ninth day (or thereabouts), they would offer you another free month.

For at least a year and a half, this is how we had internet: I would dutifully call to cancel before our thirty days were up and they would, once again, give us another free thirty days of internet. That free internet was what I built my first online businesses with—and it was a very exciting day when I finally called to cancel for good because we were making enough money from my online business to afford to pay for our internet!

Embrace the Hunt: Make Saving Money a Game, Not a Grind

One of the most powerful shifts you can make on your journey toward financial health is changing how you *think* about saving money. Instead of seeing it as something restrictive or frustrating, what if you started treating it like a game? When you make saving money something to *enjoy* rather than *endure,* it reframes your perspective.

Quick Wins Build Confidence

Savings don't have to be huge to be helpful. In fact, small wins—like saving five dollars here and seven dollars there—can build real momentum. That five-dollar coupon, that buy-one-get-one freebie, that clearance find you actually needed . . . it all adds up! And when you start to notice those little victories, you begin to realize you do have what it takes to steward your resources well.

Here are a few ideas to spark those quick wins:

- Use a cash-back app like Fetch or Ibotta when you buy groceries.
- Swap a takeout night for a freezer meal you prepped.
- Choose store-brand over name-brand for one item each week.
- Stack a digital coupon with a sale on something you *already planned to buy.*

Every time you choose a smarter option, you're flexing your frugal muscles. They get stronger with use!

When you see the progress you're making, you'll stay more motivated and have a lot more fun along the way.

Ask the Magic Question: "How Can I Get This for Less?"

Before every purchase—big or small—pause and ask yourself, *Is there a way I could get this for less?*

You don't have to become extreme or obsessive. But just by getting curious, you open the door to savings you might have overlooked.

Maybe you

- Find a coupon
- Wait for a sale

- Choose secondhand
- Earn cash back
- Buy in bulk
- Borrow or barter instead of buy

You don't have to do it all, but just asking the question can shift your mindset from *default spender* to *intentional steward*.

▸ **Tip:** We've saved thousands of dollars over the years by pausing before checkout (no matter what the purchase is) and asking, "Is this the best way to spend this money?" Sometimes the answer is yes. But many times, it leads us to a better, cheaper, or more creative option!

Final Thoughts: Keep It Joyful

Saving money doesn't have to feel like punishment. When you turn it into a challenge, a puzzle, or even a bit of a game, it becomes something *energizing* instead of exhausting.

You can do it well without doing it all. Every little win counts. Every thoughtful choice matters. And over time, those choices build a life of margin, freedom, and joy.

So go ahead: Embrace the hunt. There's fun (and savings) to be found.

Journaling Prompt

Take a moment to reflect: *What's one area where I can stop paying full price this week?* Is it groceries? A gift you need to buy? A meal out? A clothing purchase?

Write it down. Commit to a small, strategic decision. Then watch what happens—not just to your bank account, but to your confidence.

Small Wins Tracker

	Small Win	Amount Saved ($)	How it Felt
Day 1			
Day 2			
Day 3			
Day 4			
Day 5			
Day 6			
Day 7			

You're living proof that paying less *really does pay off*.

And there's one more strategy that is going to help you to stay consistent with these first six healthy habits, and we'll talk about that in the final chapter.

5 Kitchen Money-Saving Strategies That Are Totally Worth It (at Least for Me!)

One of the best ways to decide if a money-saving idea is truly worth your effort is to think of it in terms of *return on investment* (ROI). In other words, ask yourself

How much does this save me per hour?
Is that a good "hourly wage" for the time I'm putting in?
Could I spend my time on something else that saves (or earns) more?

Here's a little mindset shift I love: Every dollar you *don't* spend is tax-free. Unlike income you earn (and pay taxes on), money you save goes straight into your pocket. That means even small wins can really add up!

So what's *actually* worth your time? That's going to look different for everyone, but I thought I'd share a few of my favorite in-the-kitchen money-saving strategies that have a great return on investment for our family:

1. **Making Homemade Uncrustables—Saves about $0.80 per minute**
   My kids love Uncrustables, but the store-bought ones are pricey! I often make my own in batches and freeze them. It takes about ten minutes to whip up a dozen, and I'm easily saving $8 or more each time.
   Worth it? Absolutely! That's nearly $50 an hour in savings.
2. **Checking Grocery Store Sales Flyers—Saves $1 to $2 per minute**
   Before I shop at the grocery store, I quickly scan the weekly sales and digital coupons (if applicable). I usually save $10 to $20 just by being intentional.
   Worth it? Yes! It's such a simple way to stretch our grocery dollars.

3. **Planning Meals Around What We Already Have—Saves $1 to $2 per minute**
   Instead of starting from scratch, I look at what's in our fridge, freezer, and pantry and build our meal plan from there. It helps us waste less food and avoid unnecessary store runs.
   Worth it? 100 percent! And it keeps things from going to waste.
4. **Packing My Lunch—Saves $1 to $2 per minute**
   Taking a few minutes in the morning to pack a lunch if I am going to be out during the day saves me at least $7 to $10 every time I skip eating out. I usually do this at least once or twice a week, so this saves me at least $40 to $60 (or more!) each month!
   Worth it? Without a doubt! Plus, it's usually healthier.
5. **Meal Prepping on the Weekend—Saves $30 to $40 per hour**
   An hour or two on Sunday to chop veggies, prep proteins, or bake muffins can make our weekdays run so much more smoothly and helps us avoid the temptation of takeout.
   Worth it? Yes! It saves time and money during busy weeks.

Habit #7

Consult Your Ninety-Year-Old Self

Build Your Legacy on Change, Humility, and Hope

Imagine it's your ninetieth birthday.

The room is full of people, full of laughter, full of stories. Grandkids are giggling. Someone's playing a familiar song on the piano. The cake is your favorite, and the memories being shared bring tears to your eyes. Not because your life was perfect, but because it was intentional. You lived it on purpose, with calm and measured decision-making.

That's the perspective I want you to bring into this final habit.

Habit #7 is the thread that ties all the others together. It invites you to zoom out from the stress of today—past the budget spreadsheets, the grocery totals, and the unexpected bills—and ask a question that brings everything into clearer focus:

What will matter most when I'm ninety?

Asking this question on a regular basis will help you live today in a way that your future self will be grateful for and that those who come after you will be impacted by. When you are intentional about your finances, with an eye on what will matter most at the end of your life, it becomes about so much more than managing money; it's about shaping a legacy.

The Wisdom of Looking Ahead

In a world that encourages us to buy now and figure it out later, long-term thinking is radical. But the most meaningful financial lives aren't built on quick wins. They're built with patience, sacrifice, and vision.

That's what my parents showed me. They made a plan to pay off their mortgage, save up, and build a house debt-free, and then they stuck to it.

And while we certainly made sacrifices, there was joy in that season too. Taking cookies and lemonade to the guys working on the house. Watching the walls go up. Getting to spend hours playing on the land and exploring. Choosing the color for my room and helping to paint. We all pitched in. It was hard work. But it was rich in meaning.

My parents' financial legacy was forged through quiet faithfulness. Spending hours negotiating the best deals. Working late into the night to clean up after the contractors had left. Painting into the wee hours of the morning. It was built on the way they kept going—through storms, setbacks, sweat, and sacrifice.

And now, decades later, that legacy lives in me.

They weren't living just for the moment. They were living for something lasting. They were building not just a home but a life of intention and impact.

The Ninety-Year-Old Test: A Financial Filter

My parents' decisions and the life they have lived before me have deeply impacted the way I view money, the way I approach giving, and the daily decisions—big and small—I make when it comes to finances.

They taught me to set goals, plan for the future, work hard, make choices that would allow me to live more purposefully and give more generously, and to be faithful in my follow-through.

I remember, as a teen, watching my parents give generously to others. They paid for numerous things for friends, often anonymously. I can't tell the stories here because my parents wouldn't want anyone to know (and they probably don't even realize that I discovered multiple financial gifts they had given by something they said or a receipt I saw!), but I know they gave away thousands of dollars.

And I am positive there are many, many other times when they gave money or paid for something for someone that I don't know about. But their secret generosity that was borne from their frugality and careful management of money forever changed me. I knew that was how I wanted to live someday.

So when my husband and I set the goal of living debt-free, it wasn't just so we could be in a better financial position; it was truly so that we could give generously and freely as needs arose and our hearts were stirred.

I cannot begin to tell you the joy that comes from generosity. From living with arms open wide. From seeing ourselves as conduits of blessing to others.

Yes, it is nice to not have the strain of living paycheck to paycheck, but for us, being careful with our finances is about so much more: It's about being free to lavishly bless others. We spend carefully and save faithfully and budget meticulously, not so we can hoard up resources for our future, but so we can write a check to help change lives.

That, my friend, is the heart of financial intention. I can tell you from experience that Acts 20:35, which says "It is more blessed to give than to receive," is true. And this is what living with your ninety-year-old self in mind is all about!

For as long as I can remember, I've naturally viewed my daily choices through a long-term lens (I share more of that back story in my book *The Time-Saving Mom*). I'd often ask myself what would truly matter twenty-five years from now—or even at the end of my life—and let those answers shape my decisions.

But I never had the right words to explain this mindset or help others see life this way until a few years ago, when I sat down with my business coach, Alli Worthington, for an end-of-year meeting. As she guided me through a series of reflection questions to help me look back on the lessons of the past year and ahead to the goals for the next, something powerful happened.

In the midst of those questions, she asked, **"What would your ninety-year-old self tell you to be doing with your life right now?"**

This question stopped me in my tracks. Wait, what? I had to have her ask it again because it felt so profound. I honestly was speechless and fumbled for an answer because it caught me so off-guard.

But since that meeting many months ago, I have pondered that question over and over.

It has stuck with me, challenged me, inspired me, and motivated me to change the way I view life.

When I'm ninety, will I look back and be grateful for the decisions I'm making today? Will I be glad I spent my money the way I'm spending it right now? Are my financial goals and priorities ones that are in line with what my ninety-year-old self would encourage and agree with?

Here are some other ways to ask yourself this question and process a long-term perspective.

- If you could ask your future self for advice, what would she tell you to focus on right now?
- Imagine you're ninety years old, looking back, what would you wish you had done at this stage of your life?
- What would your older, wiser self urge you to start (or stop) doing today?
- What guidance would a letter from your ninety-year-old self include?
- What would your ninety-year-old self say matters most in this season?
- Picturing yourself decades from now, what will you be grateful you acted on today?

It's not just for big decisions like buying a house or starting a business. It's for the everyday:

- That Target run.
- That vacation we feel pressure to book.
- That "treat" that might derail our budget or our tranquility.
- That conversation we need to have about money.
- That financial decision you've been putting off.
- That idea you've been considering jumping on to put yourself in a better financial place.
- That donation you've been wanting to make.
- That friend you've been feeling inspired to help financially.

When we filter our spending and saving through the lens of our future self, we start to make choices that align with the kind of life that matters, not just with what feels convenient today.

Maybe you're thinking, *But I've already wasted years. I've made mistakes.* Let me quietly remind you: Legacy starts today. The most powerful legacies aren't built on perfection. They're built on change, humility, and hope.

Redefining Wealth Through the Eyes of Your Future Self

If your ninety-year-old self could talk to you today, I imagine she'd say

"Don't worry so much about the perfectly styled home. Focus on the memories made in it."

"Don't chase status. Cultivate peace."

"Don't spend to keep up. Spend intentionally and use your finances to make an impact."

"Don't be afraid to live simply. Choose margin and meaning."

"Don't wait to help that friend financially. Write the check today."

Wealth isn't just a number on a screen. It's the ability to live out your values. To give freely. To say no to stress and yes to calm. It's the strength to choose contentment over comparison. And the courage to raise your kids with the same mindset.

Leaving a Strong Legacy Starts When They're Little

Just as my mindsets and habits around money were shaped when I was young, it's likely yours were too. This is a good reminder that the same is true for kids today.

The way we talk about money in front of children—whether they're ours or others'—lays the foundation for how they'll view finances for life. That doesn't mean we never buy them things. But it does mean we help them see that money isn't endless. That we work for what we have. And that the wait makes the reward sweeter.

When we try to fix things for our kids without letting them problem-solve or if we never give them the opportunity to handle money or make money to pay for things themselves, we rob them of the chance to

- Learn the joy of working toward a goal
- Practice patience
- Cultivate contentment
- Grow in gratitude

It's not always easy to let them struggle a little. But it's worth it. And don't underestimate what they're capable of.

5 Money Mindsets to Teach Your Kids

You don't need a full-fledged curriculum to teach your kids financial wisdom. Just start with these five truths.

1. Everything you buy costs more than just money. It also costs time. Help them ask: *"Is this worth the hours I'll have to work for it?"*
2. Living on less than you make is a gift to your future self. Teach budgeting early and normalize planning ahead.
3. Compound interest is your friend. Encourage saving early—even small amounts make a big difference over time.
4. You won't become better with money just because you have more of it. Help them manage a little well and they'll be able to manage more wisely.
5. They are more capable than you think. Let them try. Let them fail. Let them grow through the process.

Whether it's chores, saving up for a toy, or helping with budgeting as a teen, these are not just life skills. They're seeds of resilience, responsibility, and resourcefulness.

Making It Practical: Your Ninety-Year-Old Self Checklist

If you want to begin living with legacy in mind, take a few moments to reflect.

- What do I want to remember from this season?
- What will I wish I had done more of? (Connection? Rest? Generosity?)
- What will I wish I had done less of? (Worry? Comparison? Striving?)
- What is one small shift I can make today to align with my long-term vision?
- What are three values I want to filter my financial decisions through?

  Sample financial values:
  - Contentment over comparison
  - Generosity over greed
  - Long-term gain over short-term gratification
  - Simplicity over status
  - Stewardship over splurging
  - Margin over maxing out
  - Intentionality over impulse
  - Needs over wants
  - Health over hurry
  - Freedom over fear
  - Impact over image

- Legacy over luxury
- People over things
- Peace over perfection
- Purpose over pressure

You don't need a six-figure income to leave a legacy. You just need to live with intention, one faithful choice at a time.

I opened this book by telling you about a time when we had two very young kids, a bank account that was fast dwindling, and my husband was without a job. It was a very scary time for us financially. There were so many days when panic was my constant companion. I worried about how we were going to pay our bills, how we were going to stay afloat, and what we were going to do long term if my husband didn't find a job quickly.

We had worked so hard to stay out of debt while my husband went to law school. We had already taken a very countercultural path and chosen to live extremely frugally. As I've recounted in these pages, we were on a strict written budget and accounted for every dollar spent. We shopped at thrift stores. We did without. We made do with what we had. I earned money every way I could come up with—including selling on eBay, making a little side money from blogging and affiliate marketing, mystery shopping, working as a virtual assistant, taking surveys, and even dumpster diving for coupons to play the drugstore game.

We had thought things would get better once my husband graduated from law school and he was able to work full time. But instead, he was unemployed and struggling to find another job.

It was in that place of desperation, though, that my creativity kicked into high gear. I considered all the different things I had tried to make money and decided to take what I'd learned over the last few years and attempt something new. I had learned some different ways to make money from blogging and I had been teaching my friends how to play the drugstore game. I'd also been writing a little bit about saving money on groceries on my mommy blog.

The idea came to me: What if I were to start a blog that was all about saving money? What if I took the information I was sharing with my local friends every week about where to go to get the best deals and posted it online?

I still remember sitting on the living room floor and tossing around ideas for a name when MoneySavingMom.com popped into my head. I bought the domain name, set up the blog, and announced it to the world. My hope was that it would bring in a few hundred extra dollars each month, which would be huge for our budget!

Little did I dream that the blog I started in a place of needing to do something to change our financial situation would end up completely reversing the trajectory of our family and future! Within a year, we were making a full-time income from MoneySavingMom.com, and within six years, my husband shut down the law firm he owned and came home full-time. Today, we have a team of fifteen people who help run the various aspects of the business, and I have the immense privilege of helping hundreds of thousands of families save money and live more intentionally with their finances every single day!

I look back and realize that had we not gone through that really hard season of our lives, I doubt I would have ever been inspired to start MoneySavingMom.com. You never know how God might use the difficult parts of your story as the catalyst for something that will go on to not only change your life, but possibly the lives of thousands (or even hundreds of thousands) of others!

Every time you **Start with What You Have** (Habit #1), you show that financial peace begins in the present, not "someday."

Every time you **Decide Your Financial Priorities** (Habit #2), you remind yourself (and those watching you!) that money is a tool to help you prioritize what matters most, not something to chase without purpose.

Every time you **Predetermine Your Spending** (Habit #3), you prove that a plan isn't restrictive; it's the road map to freedom.

Every time you **Use Cash for Everything** (Habit #4), you train yourself to live within your means and experience the deep satisfaction of spending money you actually have.

Every time you **Create Irresistible Accountability** (Habit #5), you make it harder to drift away from your goals and easier to keep showing up for your future self.

Every time you **Stop Paying Full Price** (Habit #6), you stretch your resources and practice the stewardship that leads to margin, generosity, and freedom.

And every time you **Consult Your Ninety-Year-Old Self** (Habit #7), you lift your eyes from the urgent to the important and you choose to intentionally write the story you want your life to tell.

Friend, these aren't just nice habits. They're *legacy* habits. They shape the way you live, give, and impact the world.

Your ninety-year-old self will thank you. Your children—or any of the people whose lives you've touched—will rise up and call you wise.

And one day, when the stories are told and the memories are shared, people will say, "She lived on purpose. She lived with peace. And she left something that lasted."

That is wealth. That is legacy. That is the beautiful life you are building—one habit, one choice, one step at a time.

No matter your current situation.

No matter your income or job.

No matter your background, education, or location.

You can live a financially healthy life.

You can flourish.

You can leave a legacy.

And I'm cheering you on every single step of the way.

Notes

Chapter 1 Habit #1: Start with What You Have

1. This saying, or wording similar to it, is often attributed to Henry Ford. You can read more about its possible origins in "Quote Origin: Whether You Believe You Can Do a Thing or Not, You Are Right," Quote Investigator, February 3, 2015, https://quoteinvestigator.com/2015/02/03/you-can/.

2. Dan Drake et al., *Building True Intimacy: Creating a Connection That Stands the Test of Time* (self-published, 2023), 88.

3. Drake et al., *Building True Intimacy*, 89.

Chapter 4 Habit #4: Use Cash for Everything

1. Robin Saks Frankel, "How Does Your Debt Compare? U.S. Credit Card Debt in 2026," *Forbes*, December 23, 2025, https://www.forbes.com/advisor/credit-cards/average-credit-card-debt/.

2. "Spend 'Til It Hurts: Researching the Pain of Paying," Carnegie Mellon University, accessed February 16, 2026, https://www.cmu.edu/homepage/practical/2007/winter/spending-til-it-hurts.shtml.

3. "Spend 'Til It Hurts," Carnegie Mellon.

4. Drazen Prelec and Duncan Simester, "Always Leave Home Without It: A Further Investigation of the Credit-Card Effect on Willingness to Pay," *Marketing Letters* 12, no. 1 (2001): 5–12, https://www.researchgate.net/publication/233496571_Always_Leave_Home_Without_It_A_Further_Investigation_of_the_Credit-Card_Effect_on_Willingness_to_Pay.

5. Sachin Banker et. al, "Neural Mechanisms of Credit Card Spending," *Scientific Reports* 11, no. 1 (2021), https://pmc.ncbi.nlm.nih.gov/articles/PMC7892835/.

6. Katherine Haan, "People Are Twice As Likely to Spend More Money When Using Card Than Cash," *Forbes*, May 16, 2024, https://www.forbes

.com/advisor/business/software/people-twice-likely-spend-using-card-than-cash/.

Chapter 5 Habit #5: Create Irresistible Accountability

1. Jeff Haden, "Want to Be More Successful? Research Shows An Accountability Buddy Makes a Huge Difference, but With 1 (Literally) Meaningful Catch," *Inc.*, February 13, 2024, https://www.inc.com/jeff-haden/want-to-be-more-successful-research-shows-an-accountability-buddy-makes-a-huge-difference-but-with-one-literally-meaningful-catch.html.

2. Reda Wigle, "Doing This Makes You More Likely to Succeed at a Fitness Goal," *New York Post*, May 1, 2024, https://nypost.com/2024/05/01/health/doing-this-makes-you-more-likely-to-succeed-at-a-fitness-goal/.

3. Howard J. Klein et al., "When Goals Are Known: The Effects of Audience Relative Status on Goal Commitment and Performance," *Journal of Applied Psychology* 105, no. 4 (2019): 372–389, https://psycnet.apa.org/record/2019-45131-001.

4. Sören Krach et al., "The Rewarding Nature of Social Interactions," *Frontiers in Behavioral Neuroscience* 4, no. 22 (2010), https://pmc.ncbi.nlm.nih.gov/articles/PMC2889690/.

CRYSTAL PAINE is a *New York Times* bestselling author, host of *The Crystal Paine Show* podcast, and founder of one of the top personal finance blogs on the web, MoneySavingMom.com. Her desire is to help women across the globe live with more joy and intention in their everyday lives. Her biggest passions are helping women understand how Jesus can radically transform their lives, raising awareness for people with disabilities, and finding great deals at the grocery store. She lives with her husband and six kids in the Nashville, Tennessee, area.

Connect with Crystal:

MoneySavingMom.com

Facebook @MoneySavingMom

Personal Instagram @TheMoneySavingMom

Deals Instagram @MSMDeals

Business Coaching Instagram @WAHMCoach